A HISTORY OF PILLING

F. J. Sobee

with a new introduction
by

Brian Marshall

Brian Marshall
November 1997

1997
Landy Publishing

A History Of Pilling by F. J. Sobee was first published in 1953. This photographic reprint, with added illustrations and a new introduction by Brian Marshall, is published in 1997 by Landy Publishing, "Acorns", 3 Staining Rise, Staining, Blackpool, FY3 0BU
Tel. & Fax: 01253 895678

ISBN 1 872895 32 8

Printed by T. Snape & Co. Ltd., Preston

Foreword to the Second Edition

It is a signal honour for me to have been invited to write the foreword to the second edition of F. J. Sobee's noted book, *A History Of Pilling*. He was a man of great stature in the village whose folk he served for more than three decades, and he is remembered by many, though it is almost 40 years since he left. To some he is the village schoolmaster, firm but fair, to others he is Commanding Officer of the local Home Guard Unit during World War II. There are those who knew him as conductor of Pilling Jubilee Silver Band or as a founder member of the Pilling Historical Society. This was a man of many parts and of boundless interests.

Frederick James Sobee was born at Rainhill in 1898. While he was still a baby the family moved to Winwick where his father, a man of Devon, was Night Supervisor at the County Asylum. Barely completing his secondary education at the Boteler Grammar School, Warrington, he volunteered at the age of seventeen and a half for service with the Manchester Regiment in the Great War. He was later commissioned and ended the war as a Lieutenant. After his military service he went to Manchester University where he graduated Bachelor of Arts in 1922. He then underwent teacher training and after just four years in schools at Warrington, was appointed in 1927 to the Headship of the Church of England School, Pilling, where he was to spend the rest of his working life.

After 31 years of devoted service to the people of Pilling, he retired in August 1958 and moved away to live at Lowton, near Warrington, not far from his birthplace. Sadly, his retirement did not last for very long. He suffered from ill health and died in October 1960 at the age of 62.

The achievement for which he is best remembered, by many who knew him, as well as by many who did not, is the publication of his book in 1953. It was an ambitious project, seeking as it did to present, in 156 pages, a survey of Pilling history from the end of the last glaciation down to the 20th. century. This broad sweep, not just of centuries but of millennia, deals with the arrival of the first human settlers during the Neolithic and follows the Pilling story through the ages, recording the doings of local folk until we come to the names of people that some of us actually knew. Part of what he records is routine, much of it is fascinating, but all of it is the very essence of good, solid local history. There are characters aplenty such as Rev. George Holden, Perpetual Curate of Pilling from 1758 to 1767, who was a noted mathematician and compiler of the first tide table for Morecambe Bay, and William Thornton, a soldier who was paraded naked before King George IV so that the sovereign might observe at first hand the most perfect specimen of manhood in the British Army.

As a leading antiquary of the area and an enthusiastic founder member of the Pilling Historical Society, he had first hand experience of the antiquities, both sites and artefacts, that feature prominently in the early chapters of the book. He was fully conversant with matters relating to the Neolithic, the Bronze Age and the Iron Age as these periods were perceived by archaeologists of the time in which he was writing. Major changes in archaeological science have taken place since then, however, most significantly perhaps, in dating techniques. Sobee refers to the first human inhabitants of Pilling at the beginning of the Neolithic, to which he ascribes a date of 2500 B.C. In 1953 this was the accepted date for the arrival of these early farmers in Britain, but during the intervening decades, major scientific developments, particularly in the fields of *radiocarbon dating,* and of *dendrochronology (*tree ring dating) have pushed back dates by more than a millennium, and estimates nearer to 4,000 B.C. are now frequently made for early Neolithic finds.

Mr. Sobee would be more concerned though with the archaeological discoveries that have taken place in Pilling itself since he wrote his book. Waiting to be discovered under the ground were at least two major sites, over which he, like countless others, had probably walked, never suspecting their presence. The first of these to be unearthed was the site near Fluke Hall which made the national headlines when it came to light in 1970. This is the so-called *'Pilling Enigma'*, large numbers of rectangular pits measuring roughly 6 feet by 2 feet and varying in depth between 3 and 7 feet. Initially assumed to be graves, it was soon evident that this was probably not the case as none of those examined contained any suggestion of a burial. Their purpose and date of origin have remained a mystery throughout the 26 years that have elapsed since their discovery, a mystery that has been compounded by subsequent discoveries of identical pits, at Preesall in one direction and Cockerham in the other. This has led to the suggestion that there may be a continuous chain of these pits close to the shore and extending for four or five miles. Many theories as to the purpose of the pits have been advanced, the most recent, and perhaps most accurate of which is by Mr. Headlie Lawrenson, President of the Pilling Historical Society and another of its founder members. He proposes a chain or belt of defensive pits, covered with matting or brushwood and furnished with sharpened stakes in the bottom, constructed by the Romans to provide some sort of protection for a highly vulnerable stretch of coastline against a sudden sea-borne incursion. Such an attack, by Irish raiders, was indeed a possibility during the later part of the Roman period, and defences of this type are well documented on other Roman sites in Britain.

iv

Probably of greater importance than the 'graves,' is the Bronze Age habitation she excavated near Bradshaw Lane in 1980 which was evidently a homestead of the later Bronze Age c. 1000-700 B.C.. Of particular interest on the site were a number of pieces of amber, a substance much prized in the ancient world and one that does not occur in Britain. A likely place of origin for this is the Baltic and its presence on a Pilling site says much about patterns of trade three thousand years ago. Sobee writes of the expansion of the moss, a process that was brought about by the major climatic change of around 500 B.C. when the mild, dry conditions of the Sub-Boreal phase gave way to the cool, wet Atlantic phase. No better evidence for such expansion could be found than the site at Bradshaw Lane, where a homestead, occupied for generations, was engulfed around this time by the ever spreading moss and was to remain under the peat until a date virtually within living memory.

The local discoveries that Mr. Sobee would have observed with the keenest of interest are those recently made at Nateby, where it begins to appear that finds of the Neolithic, the Iron Age, and the Roman Period, still in the early stages of investigation, will come to be regarded as of major importance.

When it was first published some 43 years ago, F. J. Sobee's, *A History of Pilling*, quickly established itself as a classic of local history. It was widely read in the district and its scholarship and erudition were much admired. The author's deep regard for, and grasp of, his subject are plain to see and he has produced a work which has stood the test of time. That it is being republished after the passing of so many years is testimony to its enduring qualities. Those who read it when it first appeared will find it as fresh and as relevant as it was in 1953, while those encountering it for the first time will discover a gem that may well demand a further edition in another 43 years.

During the production of this second edition it has been necessary to seek the help of a considerable number of people to whom grateful thanks are due. These include: Messrs. Edward and Alan Sobee, sons of the author, for family detail and permission to publish; Mrs. Sophia Sherdley, Mr. John Higginson, Mr. Headlie Lawrenson and numerous others in Pilling and district who have loaned photographs for use in this edition or have given freely of their time in order to assist, advise and generally to encourage.

Brian Marshall
Knott End
July 1997

v

BROADFLEET, PILLING.

A HISTORY OF PILLING

DEDICATED

TO

THE PEOPLE OF PILLING

PREFACE

In the year 1858, the Rev. J. D. Banister wrote : " Every district in our highly favoured land affords some peculiarity worthy of note, and the changes that have occurred in by-gone times, or those occurring in our own may be deeply interesting, if not to ourselves now, at least will be to posterity. If records of interesting facts occurring in every parish had been made and carefully preserved, what a fund of information would have been at the command of the modern historian. A history of England drawn from such sources would have commanded more attention from the masses of the present intelligent age than all the fine spun theories of historians. Facts should ever be the sure foundation of all history."

How true ! I have continually borne in mind this last sentence and have rarely ventured to express an opinion. My search has been for facts and I have recorded facts. This book is not intended to be a literary work, but rather one to which the reader may refer for information. I have written it from a historian's point of view. It seemed to me to be my duty to undertake this work as in the course of my various offices, I have had access to documents to which others have not.

If the reader derives a fraction of the pleasure from reading as I have had from writing, and if I have succeeded in strengthening the love and pride of the present and future generations of Pilling in their village, that is the only reward I ask.

F. J. SOBEE,

Pilling.   *January*, 1953

FOREWORD

by

REV. I. O. EVANS, *Vicar of Pilling*

In the " Lay of the Last Minstrel," Sir Walter Scott wrote :—
" Breathes there the man with soul so dead,
Who never to himself hath said
This is my own, my native land."

It is such pride in one's own place which has inspired the author to write this book, and doubtless will stimulate Pillingers to read it with great interest.

For some years Mr. F. J. Sobee has been engaged in careful research, a whole day might be spent at a Records Office with negative results, on another day he would be rewarded by finding the documentary evidence he sought. His many acknowledgments indicate his own labours in the search for material. And here we have the result. It is a local history and therefore must make a strong appeal to local people.

Also, by the modern conception of history, this book is a valuable contribution to the history of the country.

To quote G. K. Chesterton : " Villages are, in a real sense, the Crown Jewels ; they are the national, the English, the un- replaceable things."

Well ! Here we have the history of one village. A book to read — and study ; a book worthy to pass down to future generations.

CONTENTS

ACKNOWLEDGMENTS

I wish to acknowledge my indebtedness to Mr. R. Sharpe-France, Archivist to the Lancashire County Council, who encouraged me to carry out this work and gave me every assistance possible, advising me, passing on information and giving me access to documents at the Record Office and allowing me to publish extracts from his book *The Plague in Lancashire*, from which I have taken much of the information in Chapter 6 ; also transcriptions of Quarter Sessions Petitions and the photograph of the letter to the Justices of Peace.

To the Staff at the Record Office, also, I wish to acknowledge my appreciation of many kindnesses shown to me.

To the Chetham Society my gratitude is due for permission to publish extracts from their publications, particularly *The Cockersand Chartulary*.

The members of the Pilling Historical Society have rendered invaluable assistance in field work, and have derived considerable enjoyment from it. What exciting times we have had ! My thanks are due to them for permission to publish extracts from their Reports and findings.

Antiquarians in general owe a debt to Mr. W. C. Armer and Mr. T. Ronson for their assistance and co-operation in the investigations on " Kate's Pad."

Thanks to Mr. S. Kellet for his interest in the excavations of the old chapel.

To Drs. E. M. M. Alexander and P. Lasko, of the British Museum, I owe a great debt of gratitude for identifying and giving their opinions on objects which have had a very important bearing on the story of Pilling.

Mr. D. Walker, of Cambridge University, has kindly allowed me to print extracts from his Report on the Pollen Analysis at the site of Kate's Pad. More than that, he has taught me to regard the peat not merely as combustible material, but as an organism with a wonderful story to tell.

The Vicar, The Rev. I. O. Evans, The Pilling Parochial Church Council, The Managers of the Church of England School, and the Trustees of the Carter's Charity and the Parish Council have been most helpful in allowing me access to their archives and placing books, documents, and Registers at my disposal.

Thanks to Mr. R. E. Shepherd for information on the Garstang Knott End Railway.

The proprietors of *The Lancaster Guardian* have very kindly allowed me to use articles on the Wesleyan Methodist movement, which have appeared in *The Lancaster Guardian.*

I am indebted to Miss D. M. Phillips for permission to publish her poem on " The Marsh," and to Miss C. Banister for her support and the loan of papers, which belonged to her grandfather, Rev. J. D. Banister.

Mr. H. Curwen and Mr. F. J. Gornall have kindly given me permission to publish their photographs and have given me indispensable help and advice with my photography. I regret I have have not been able to trace the photographers of some of the old photographs I have copied. I freely acknowledge my indebtedness and if I have infringed copyright, I crave pardon.

To Mr. J. Turnbull, thanks for carrying out the onerous task of reading through my script.

I wish to thank my many Pilling friends, who have given me all the support possible, loaning papers, giving me information and above all, giving me encouragement.

Finally, to all Subscribers, thanks for their generous co-operation in making it possible to publish this book and to the Publishing Committee for relieving me of the responsible task of financing and getting the work printed and published—Councillor R. Rossall, J.P., Rev. I. O. Evans, Councillor J. B. Clarkson, Mr. J. Hall, Rev. Father J. Hardman, Mr. W. Jenkinson, Mr. J. Gornall, Rev. R. F. Cookson, Miss C. Corless, and Mr. E. Hodgson.

To one and all—my sincere thanks.

F.J.S.

CHAPTER 1

The Early Story of the Township of Pilling

PILLING is a small township, with a population of 1,444 (1931 Census) and an area of 6,003 statute acres, tucked away in a southern corner of Morecambe Bay. It is a tiny remnant of old Britain ; an independent entity cut off from the rest of England for more than 2,000 years by the sea and the bog ; until recently rich in dialect and folklore ; a bird sanctuary and a happy hunting ground for the botanist and the lover of nature ; with wild untouched expanses of moss, marsh and shore, each anxious to tell its story to help build up the whole.

We might commence this story at the final recession of the ice from these parts in the Daniglacial Period, that is about 18,000 B.C.—the end of the Ice Ages in England.

The ice left plenty of evidence behind. Here we find stones large and small, brought down from the North—granite from Shap, Skiddaw, Eskdale, Loch Doon ; shale from Borrowdale ; sandstone from St. Bees ; limestone from Furness ; porphyry from the Southern Uplands of Scotland. These erratics are to be seen at Eagland Hill, Bone Hill, Black Hill and the shore. On some of the larger stones scratches or striations can be clearly seen. The ice spread from glaciers in Scotland and the Lake District. It moved slowly down, bringing stones with it and grinding some into powder which forms the reddish clay called marl. There is not much of this clay on the surface in Pilling, but it can be clearly seen at Island Farm at Nateby and there are beds of this boulder clay at Eagland Hill. It often contains pebbles. It sets very hard when dry and until quite recently was used to make the floors of the cottages.

Both red and blue clay have been dug out when sinking wells. The red is formed from red sandstone and the blue from shale.

Over Pilling the ice was probably several hundred feet thick. This invasion of the ice has had a great influence on the story of Pilling. When it melted, small hills of gravel and sand were left behind. They are known as " drumlins " and we can see them stretching in a line from Crookabreast Farm, Cogie Hill, Black Lane Head, across to Kentucky and Bone Hill, south to Eagland Hill, west to Lousanna and Friar's Hill (near Moss Cottage), on to Hales' Hall and Stalmine.

Some of these hills, as is proved by the stone and bronze implements which have been found there, were no doubt sites of

1. Stone Hand Axe found
   at Bone Hill.

3. Flint and Stone Axes found at Bradshaw Land.

2. Neolithic Axe found at
   Black Lane Head.

4. Stone Adze found in the field
   North of Bradshaw Lane Farm.

very early settlements. After the ice had retreated, the rivers washed down soil from the hills and levelled up the depressions. But again the land sank slightly. Under the peat is a stratum of grey estuarine clay, in places up to fifteen feet thick. This is silt brought down by the rivers. It is usually deposited where the fresh water of the river meets the salt water of the sea. This proves, without doubt, that this land was once the estuary of one or more rivers. It is quite feasible that the River Wyre emptied into the sea here and has since changed its course. It may have joined up with the River Lune, or indeed, there might have been another river which has since disappeared. There are definite traces of an ancient river, which, however, is of later date than the clay but prior to the peat, running from Throstle Nest Farm in Winmarleigh, passing just North of Crookabreast Farm and Cogie Hill, across to Bone Hill, and possibly on to Stalmine, where it might have joined up with the River Wyre. The bed is about thirty yards wide and is composed of water-worn pebbles and is clearly visible where the dykes are cut through it.

But to return to our clay. Under the grey clay is sand which contains shells, proving that this was an ancient sea bed. Any form of glacial animal life, such as the Irish elk, must be sought under the clay. Many antlers and bones of *red* deer have been found *in* the clay.

The Rev. J. D. Banister, Curate of Pilling from 1825 to 1876, wrote : " In the whole of the district from Wyre to the Cocker the horns and bones of red deer have been met with (he tried hard to establish the existence of the *Irish elk*, but failed) when deep clay pits have been made for the cultivation of the land, or water courses have been deeply made or wells sunk into this stratum of blue (? grey) clay. In the deeping of the main drain from the mosses and low lands near Jarvis Carr, these organisms abound. In a space of about 2 yards by 2½ or 3 yards, nineteen horns of the red deer, besides skulls, leg and thigh bones and ribs, were cut out of this stratum of blue (? grey) silt. These had probably been washed by the tidal waters into a lower hollow."

His theory may, of course, be correct. Had the bones been near the top of the clay it might have been suggested that they had been put there by human beings, either discarded after eating the flesh or a hoard to trade for flint weapons when stag horns were used as picks, but up to the present time no evidence of human beings has been found *in* the clay. Quite a number of stags' horns have been found fairly recently in the region south of Head Dyke and Pear Tree Farm and Bradshaw Lane. Mr. Hodgson found one at a depth of 9 feet in the clay when digging a well in a field off Bradshaw Lane.

Some two or three thousand years B.C. the land rose relatively slightly again, and a forest began to grow. It covered a large extent in the south-eastern portion of this region. It was very

1. Bronze Spear
found at Cogie Hill.

2. Bronze Scabbard,
1st Century A.D.

3. Stone Hammer found at
Bradshaw Lane.

4. Saxon Bead found
at Newers Wood.

thick. Mr. J. Lawrenson of Cumming Carr Farm took out three hundred " stocks " in ten acres of ground in one year, and has since removed many hundreds. It was composed of oak, yew, silver birch and hazel. Where the trees have grown on the " ravin " (glacial debris of sand and gravel) the roots are much larger than those grown on the grey clay. Some of the trees are of immense size.

As for the destruction of this forest, the old theory put forward was that it was blown down by a terriffic North-westerly gale, perhaps accompanied by an inundation of the sea, and this caused the streams to be dammed up with a consequent loss of drainage, which caused water-loving plants to grow and form the moss. To support this theory it is stated that the tree trunks lie in a north-west-south-east direction as they do on Marton Moss. But any Pilling man who has seen or dug out these stocks will say this is not correct. The tree trunks lie in every direction. Admitted that some have been bent over, especially on the Winmarleigh Moss.

A more probable explanation is, we are told by the botanists, that about 600 B.C. there was a great deterioration in the climate of Britain. Conditions became very wet and Pilling, already being low-lying, the soil would become water-logged. This would be detrimental to the trees, they would die or the roots be unable to grip in the mud, but water-loving plants would grow, and so the peat would be formed. This is borne out by the fact that the roots of the trees are either lying just on top of the clay or embedded in it and surrounded by the " carr." The carr is composed very largely of giant rush (phragmites) which grows in wet conditions, indicating swamp conditions when the forest was destroyed. A point worth noting is that at Bone Hill and Lousanna there are roots but no trunks. They may have been removed for some purpose, perhaps centuries later, as the trees would continue to grow on the higher land.

The story of the people of Pilling really begins when this forest was flourishing, in the early Neolithic age, that is about 2500 B.C. The evidence is in the implements found. This area is quite rich in stone artifacts, all found *under* the peat.

There seems to be no doubt that some of the higher spots were the sites of very early settlements. They might have been seasonal settlements to which the people came down from the Pennine hills to hunt and fish and catch wild fowl, but it seems more probable they were permanent settlements. Up to the present time four stone polishers and ten stone weapons are known to have been found, and more may come to light. This seems too large a number for people living in temporary settlements to lose. No, it is more probable it was the other way round—the people went *up* the hills to worship. On our eastern flank is Crookabreast Farm, where a neolithic stone axe (now in Preston museum) and four polishers were found (one is now in Preston museum, two are in the possession of the author, and Mr. Jenkinson of Crookabreast has one). An interesting point is that one of the polishers had been pushed into a cavity among the roots at the base of an oak tree as if the owner had intended returning. The others were scattered around between the tree roots.

Another extremely interesting and important point is, the finding of these polishers proves that some of the stone axes were actually made here and were not all imported. The polishers were used to rub the stone axes into shape and polish them. Sand and water were used. A stone as near as possible to the desired shape would be found on one of the gravel hills and then the rubbing commenced. What patience and skill were necessary ! And what beautiful works of art they produced. Two perfect specimens of neolithic implements were found in the field between Cogie Hill and Black Lane Head, one by Mr. E. Myerscough (now in the possession of the author) an adze, beautifully balanced, 6 ins. long and 2½ ins. wide and 1½ ins. at the thickest part. It is made of volcanic tuff and was almost certainly brought from Langdale Pike, where there was a factory, possibly in an unfinished state. It is very similar to that found at Crookabreast.

The other, an axe, 9 ins. long by 3½ ins. wide and 1¾ ins. at the thickest part, was in the possession of Mrs. R. Slater. It is made of a hard Lake District igneous rock, partly polished. One cannot look at these axes but with a deep sense of admiration for the men who made them. No ! They were not uncouth barbarians but highly skilled men with a highly developed sense for artistic beauty and symmetry.

At Bone Hill, Mr. R. Lawson found in 1940 a small hand axe, 3 ft. deep in the gravel, when digging a water pipe track for the Imperial Chemical Industries Co. It dates from 2500—2000 B.C. and strangely is similar to a type found in Ireland. This conjures up all kinds of interesting questions. Was it made in Ireland ? If so, how had it found its way to Pilling ? Was it traded, and if so for what ? Does it suggest some form of commerce between Pilling and Ireland ? Here, also, was found in 1856 the " foundation of an ancient habitation " of circular shape, consisting of a trench 4 yds. in diameter and 20 ins. deep and 18 ins. wide. The clay, which had been dug out, had been thrown inside. Some charcoal and pieces of wood, and some hazel and alder poles, and hazel nuts were found, but there is not sufficient evidence to fix the date. The date when it was found, 1856, suggests it was the Rev. J. D. Banister who reported the find, and it is quite safe to say he would definitely make an examination on the spot, as he was a very enthusiastic antiquarian, very thorough and keen on details. Moreover, he was very well acquainted with the peat. He would, therefore, be able to pass a considered opinion as to whether the foundations were ancient or not, and his opinion is well worth while considering seriously.

Passing on to Bradshaw Lane, Mr. J. Lawson found two axes*, one an ordinary type 6 ins. long and 2½ ins. wide for insertion through the haft, made from a dark, hard mud stone, the other a neolithic flint axe. Again, the question arises, how did a flint axe come to Pilling ? The nearest place where flint is found is North Wales or in Ireland in County Antrim. Obviously, it points to trade with the outside world. While on the subject of flint, mention should be made of the finding of a small scraper in the third field west of the Church of England school in the summer of 1951 by Harold Whiteside. The farmer, Mr. H, Whiteside, had ploughed to a depth of 14 ins.

An ancient canoe, made of wood, was found at Well House Farm in 1906, when digging a well. Pieces of the canoe were in the possession of Mr. Burrows, of Poulton, and another portion was used as a post at Well House, but it has disappeared. It is possible that portions still lie buried. On the 15th and 26th May, 1951, members of the Pilling Historical Society excavated several yards round the well, but only fragments were found, but this is important as it does confirm the existence of the canoe.

We now come to the " Bronze Age." It is difficult to fix a date when the people, who introduced weapons made of bronze, first came to Britain, but it seems somewhere about 2000—1800 B.C. is an approximate date, but the development took many hundreds of years, as did the transition from stone weapons to bronze. Indeed, for many centuries, both stone and bronze weapons were used contemporaneously. But the stone axes become more of a hammer type, pierced by a hole through which the shaft was inserted. The hole was drilled by twisting a stick in the hands and using water and sand as an abrasive.

Two of these hammers* were found near where Pea Hall wood stood, by Mr. R. Gornall. Another* was found somewhere in the vicinity of Bradshaw Lane. Another, smaller*, was found by Mr. John Rossall, when mowing in a field next to Bradshaw Lane Farm and north of it. It has been described as an adze. It could have been used for this purpose, to hack out the charcoal when burning out their canoes. Or, it might have been used as a hoe. If so, it is very important, as it would point to some agriculture having been carried out in Pilling in very early days, but at the same time it could have served as a handy little battle hammer.

From stone we pass to bronze and so retrace our steps to Bone Hill. On 5th June, 1851, the Rev. W. Thornber stated (see the Lancs. and Cheshire Historical Society publications) ; " Under Bone Hill we meet with many remains, but I will particularise two arrow heads and another spear that lay not far distant from a dozen of what may be called shafts which taper to a point—I call them shafts because they had been worked with a tool. Here

All these axes marked *, with the exception of one found by Mr. R. Gornall, are in St. Michael's Museum.

too, was discovered a battle axe. It is of pale brass, mixed with much lead or tin, and flat. It weighs 23 ozs. and is in length 7½ ins., whilst at the other end the breath of it is 4½ ins. and the other 1¼ ins. The thickest part is ⅜ in. in the middle, but it tapers to sharpness at both ends."

He gives a drawing of the axe, which was of the latter part of the Early Bronze Age. The Rev. W. Thornber was friendly with the Rev. J. D. Banister and seems to have derived his information from him. We infer the axe was in the possession of the Rev. J. D. Banister, but where it is now is not known.

On our way we have passed over a field south of Cumming Carr Farm, where Mr. Tom Watson found a bronze axe (palstave) when ploughing after he and Mr. James Lawrenson had removed the tree roots. This palstave, now in the Harris Museum, is very important, as it helps us to date the peat. It was found under or very near the bottom of the peat. It is flanged and has a partial " stop." It is of the late Middle or early Late Bronze Age, that is about 1000 B.C., or perhaps a couple of centuries later.

Another bronze palstave was found by Mr. T. Hodgson in the third field south-west of Stafford's Farm. From his description it was very similar to that found at Cumming Carr. It was found about a foot above the clay. In addition, about 30 yards away, he found a stone quern and stone for grinding. These were at Brook Hall for many years. The quern was used as a stepping stone when drawing water for the cattle from the Pool (it is probably still buried there). The round stone was used to block a hole in a drain and is now under a concrete floor.

In Eight Acre field charcoal was found in the peat. Mr. W. C. Armer also found charcoal in the peat in the third field from the junction of the road running from Garstang Road to the track joining Stafford's Farm to Cumming Carr Farm.

On the 12th and 19th May, 1951, members of the Pilling Historical Society investigated a site in the second field due east of Bradshaw Lane Farm. They found a circle of stones, many broken, about 8 ft. in diameter. The stones had, without any doubt, been broken by man. Lying on the stones, which were fire-blackened, was a quantity of charcoal. There is no question of this being part of a forest fire, as the spot was localised and other trial diggings made and no more charcoal was found. One of the stones was rectangular in shape and showed definite signs of rubbing.

The stones, which were of glacial origin, had been gathered and seemed to form a floor on the damp peat, of which there were 4 to 6 ins. The site, which was on the edge of the forest, is on a slight eminence of the clay, which is 18 ins. lower at 7 yds. distance and shows a thin layer of black mud which might mark the edge of a lake or stream. There is no doubt it was the site of a human habitation in the Bronze Age, of a fairly long duration, as is proved by the thorough burning of the stones. They had, moreover, chosen as dry a spot as possible on the edge of the forest.

A bronze sword, 27½ ins. long, is said to have been found at Copthorne, but nothing definite is known about it.

At Cogie Hill was found an oak chest in which were eight socketed celts of very fine workmanship, a small spearhead about 8 ins. long, and another spearhead 18 ins. long and 3¾ ins. broad. These are all of the Late Bronze Age and one cannot help wondering at the skill and artistic sense of the men who made them. There is also a peculiarly shaped dagger or knife. It is thought by some to have been used during religious rites, perhaps by a Druid priest. That there were druids in the Fylde there is no doubt.

All these bronze weapons are in the Warrington Museum. They were presented by Lord Winmarleigh, who had a mansion in Warrington.

There is one other find to record. In 1900 Messrs. Jenkinson uncovered a semi-circle of cobble stones at Birk's Farm, Eagland Hill. It was about 7 ft. in diameter and was found at the base of an oak tree, when the peat had been removed. This might have been used for religious purposes.

During the Late Bronze Age, Britain was invaded by people from the continent of Europe known as Celts. They came in a number of waves with various dialects, among which we can distinguish the " Goidels " ; these later became the Gaels of Ireland and Scotland. The later waves of people were known as " Brythons " or " Brythonic Celts," whose language survives as modern Welsh, and it is with these people that we in Pilling are very directly concerned, for it was they who gave Pilling its name.

The name " Pilling " is derived from Celtic " *pyll* " meaning a creek, and " ing " a diminutive. Place names are a book which we can read, and contain important historical evidence.

Celtic names are unusually numerous in the Fylde, proving there must have been many Celtic settlements and, moreover, they must have survived later invasions of Romans, Norse and Anglo-Saxons, as the place names have survived, probably due to the fact that the land had become marshy and their settlements would be naturally strongly defended and difficult to get at. Other Celtic names in this district are Morecambe from *mawr* meaning great and *cam*, winding or bent ; Wyre from *gwyr* meaning pure ; Cocker meaning winding, Preesall from *prys* or *pres* meaning brushwood (all is from later Norse *agh* or *haughr* meaning a mound or hill) ; also Eccleston and Inskip probably are derived from the Celtic.*

About 500 B.C. the use of iron was introduced into Britain but throughout the country finds of ironwork have not been very rich, probably owing to the fact that iron rusts.

Here in Pilling, in the moss, was found the beautiful bronze

*—See the Chapter on Place Names of the Fylde by Dr. Ekwall in the British publication, " A Scientific Survey of Blackpool and District."

scabbard, which is at present in the Harris Museum at Preston. It is very well-known and is a classic example of bronze work during the late Iron Age.

Until evidence is forthcoming to disprove it, we are bound to include the " Kate's Pad " in this period. Dr. H. Godwin, in a letter to the author, said : " I think that it is much more likely to be much older than either Mediaeval or Roman times."

During the summer of 1949, Mr. D. Walker of the University Sub-Department of Quarternary Research, Cambridge, made an examination of the peat in Pilling, and carried out a pollen analysis on the peat at " Kate's Pad " and reported as follows : " So far as ascribing a definite date to Kate's Pad is concerned, much remains to be done, and at least one other pollen diagram for a site where a local pollen rain is not so confusing, must be prepared. At present, all that can be said is that it would appear to be risky in the extreme to suggest a very modern date (e.g. Roman or post-Roman) for Kate's Pad, the age of which is possibly much greater."

This " Pad " is a wooden track which runs through the peat. At present, it is located at Iron House Farm, Out Rawcliffe, but probably at one time it commenced somewhere south of Scronkey. In papers to the Historic Society of Lancashire and Cheshire, Vol. 1851, the Rev. W. Thornber says : " The Danes' (Kate's) Pad is formed of riven oak trees laid upon sleepers through which by square holes the planks are staked into the ground. Sometimes it is composed of one huge tree, at others of two or three, and its width varies from 20 ins. to something more. It has been traced by Mr. Banister and myself for a mile and a half into the interior of the moss. At the supposed terminus of this pad is a field completely full of holes called by Mr. Thompson, the owner, ' Penny Holes,' because the labourers, he says, had a penny a piece for the making of them to cultivate the moss with the clay."

This field is still known as " Penny Platt," and the holes are still clearly evident. It is the corner field at New Hall Farm. There is every reason to believe the story of how the field got its name is quite correct. The Rev. J. D. Banister is credited with the statement that the track consisted " of a narrow bridge of rudely riven oak trees, all literally scooped out like spouts by long usage and lying on cross sleepers alternately pegged through them in the centre of a twelve foot deposit of peat."

Unfortunately, it is difficult to sort out the truth from wishful thinking in the Rev. W. Thornber's statements. The sketch accompanying his papers to the Historic Society is just pure imagination, so we must turn to the Rev. J. D. Banister for confirmation. It would be interesting to know how he and Mr. Banister traced the track for a mile and a half, especially in the centre of a 12 ft. deposit of peat (that would be before the peat was drained and it settled down) when eight members of the Pilling Historical Society spent two long afternoons in tracing 70 yds. under ideal conditions and the soil only 18 ins. deep. Their findings did not entirely agree with those of the two Reverend gentlemen, but it is quite possible the character of the track has changed from the site where they saw it a hundred years ago.

They are embodied in the following report :—

REPORT ON INVESTIGATIONS ON " KATE'S PAD " CARRIED OUT
    BY MEMBERS OF PILLING HISTORICAL SOCIETY ON
        THE 2ND, 9TH AND 16TH SEPTEMBER, 1950.

The part of the track which was uncovered or traced is situated in two fields on Moss Cottage Farm. It consists of riven oak trees, up to 17 ft. in length, varying in width from 15 ins. to 8 ins. The trees seem to have been split into three.

1. Evidently timber was scarce, otherwise the people who laid the track would not have taken the trouble to split the trunks into three, they would have simply thrown the trunks down or been content to split them into two.

2. Four of the pieces of timber had rectangular holes cut in them, in one case sloping from 5 ins. by 3½ ins. to 2½ ins. by 1½ ins. The hole was very cleanly cut, apparently by a chisel-shaped instrument. In one case, only, a groove had been cut in the end.

3. DEPTH. In one field the track is 3 ft. below the surface, but in the next, where the top soil has been drained and cultivated and sunk, it is only 18 ins. below.

4. Axe cuts were clearly visible, and, what is very important, an axe with a straight edge, 2½ ins. across had apparently been used. This might point to it having been made of iron.

5. DIRECTION. The track at this point and from where it was last seen sóme years ago, runs in a South-Westerly direction towards a gravel hill, which is some 10 or 12 ft. higher than the surrounding country and a hundred yards across, and sometimes known as " Friar's Hill." Mr. T. Ronson, the farmer who lives at Moss Cottage Farm, states that it has been seen in a field south of Hornby Road, even closer to the hill, which is a Drumlin left by the ice. Also he states the track has been seen approximately three-quarters of a mile due south of Friar's Hill, north of Bull Foot Cottage, which also stands on a hill. This is significant. The Rev. W. Thornber stated it ran in the direction of Hales Hall. This has, therefore, yet to be proved.

6. The track does not run quite straight but bends very slightly westerly, and is somewhat erratic, but where it does bend the makers seem to have gone to some trouble to diminish the risk of falling off by trimming the ends and placing them in juxtaposition and in one case they had even gone to the trouble of placing a short length of wood 2 ft. 6 ins. by 9 ins. by 2 ins. at the bend as if to prevent a false step into the morass.

7. Remarkably, places were encountered which were, even at

[Photo by F. J. Gornall.

Kate's Pad

The Peat, Bradshaw Lane.

the present time, wetter than others and in one wet spot the oak track was laid on a piece of silver birch 4 ft. long and 4½ ins. in diameter, and on the end of an oak branch 7 in. in diameter and 6 ft. long. At other points there were quantities of birch brushwood laid down, proving that these spots were wetter when the track was laid.

8. A noticeable feature was that the track lies on heather in places but is generally embedded in a layer, approximately 3 ins. to 4 ins. thick, of giant rush only slightly decomposed (which indicates wet conditions with quick growth) pointing to the fact that the track made its way through the giant rush and would be quite hidden by them.

9. A very careful examination was made but no trace of any pegs inserted into the holes at the ends of the timbers could be found.

10. It would have been very precarious walking on this track except in bare feet. One piece of timber was only 8 ins. in diameter. In some cases the round side was uppermost and in others the flat side. Not the slightest trace of any wear was seen.

11. There appeared to have been no movement of the timbers either vertically or laterally since the track was laid.

12. About 70 yds. of the track was traced.

What the purpose of this track was it is only possible to hazard a guess. It might have lead to some kind of pier at Scronkey where it would have been possible to board the canoes and sail down Broadfleet River (Pilling Water) to the sea to fish or gather shell fish, and it might have been used as a means of communication with the outside world. Still more likely it might have lead to a settlement of refuge on the hill known as Friars' Hill.

Whatever its purpose it was a work of some magnitude. If we assume there was a minimum of a mile of track, at a very conservative estimate, more than a hundred trees would be required and these would have to be dragged from considerable distances, perhaps from Bone Hill. Would this explain why there are only roots and no trunks at Bone Hill, Lousanna, etc. ? Timber was scarce and would only be found on the higher ground where it would continue to grow after the onset of fen conditions. Also the trees had to be split and placed in position. This would require some manpower, and was without doubt intended to be for permanent use.

Before the Romans came the North of England, i.e. Yorkshire, Northumberland, Westmorland, Cumberland, Lancashire, as far north as the Caledonian Forest, was inhabited by a powerful race of people known as the " Brigantes." A sub-tribe of these, who lived in this district, was the Setantii or Segantii. Sir J. Rhys*

* "Celtic Britain "—Rhys. S.P.C.K.

says the Segantii may have been so named from their living near the Segeia or Seteia River, which is supposed to have been the Mersey. Segeia was most likely not so much the name of the river as the divinity of the river.

Another suggestion is that Setantii or Segantii means " The dwellers in the country of the water." Most of the low-lying parts of the Fylde at that time were undoubtedly morass, and would provide excellent places of refuge. Several canoes made of light wooden framework, covered with hide were found at Marton Mere.

Their religion was Druidical. The Rev. W. Thornber says : " An ornament called a ' Druid's Egg ' was found at Mill Hill, near Kirkham. Of all the relics found here the most singular and curious is a druid's egg or amulet in excellent preservation. It is a ring of light green glass, roped by a cord of blue, which is wrapped thus by a thread of white. From its having been much worn in the centre, it must have been suspended from the neck as a charm."

This description seems to fit almost exactly with that of the Saxon bead found in the moat surrounding the site of the old chapel (see chapter 2). Pliny tells us that the Druids had certain stones called "snakes' eggs." One of which he saw was as big as a medium-sized apple. They were probably the fossils of sea urchins, which were held in veneration. Small ones were sometimes perforated and hung round the neck as beads or charms. Thornber may, however, be correct, as later thick glass beads were used. These were called " adder stones " and have been found in barrows of an early date. " Druid's eggs " were worn by the priests only. If there were priests there must have been a fair number of people in this area.

Dr. Jackson discovered a Bronze Age burial circle at Bleasdale on the hillside.

Did our ancestors use the tracks through the moss to go to Bleasdale to worship on special occasions, or did they have a sacred spot at Eagland Hill too ? In the field north-west of Tarn Farm, Eagland Hill, there is a hill composed of glacial gravel, and on this hill is an area of ground approximately 70 yds. across on which is (1952) a large number of tree roots almost exclusively yew. In the writer's opinion they might have been deliberately planted to form a sacred grove. In pre-Christian times yew trees were sacred and regarded as a symbol of immortality and were planted on religious sites. Julius Caesar tells us the Druids preached immortality, and it is generally accepted that it was they who adopted the yew as a sacred symbol of immortality. It was, however, regarded as a sacred tree in Britain even before Druidical times. Oak trees grew in profusion around this site, some of immense size. One at the foot of the hill measured 60 ft. to the lowest branch, and a quantity of charcoal was found at the base.

As mentioned in a later chapter, the name Eagland Hill comes from the old Norse " Eiki Lundr," which means an oak grove. A " lund " was a sacred grove where pagan rites were carried out, and although the Norsemen did not appear on the scene until almost a thousand years later, it seems reasonable to conjecture that pagan worship might have been carried on at Eagland Hill for some centuries after the advent of the Romans, and later, Christianity might have been stamped out or driven underground by the Norse and pagan worship reintroduced. The yew trees, of course, would have gone, but there would, no doubt, be oak trees on the higher ground.

It is very speculative, but then we might mention again the peculiarly shaped knife, which was found among the Cogie Hill hoard and which some antiquarians think might have been used by a Druid priest when conducting religious ceremonies.

Then came the Romans. They did not get on very fast in conquering the Brythons or Britons. It was a continuous struggle for at least two hundred years to hold them down. In the year 208 A.D. Severus came to Britain. Some antiquarians endeavour to make him responsible for constructing " Kate's Pad," quoting Herodian as saying, " He, Severus, more especially endeavoured to make the marshy places stable by means of causeways, that his soldiers treading with safety, might pass them, and having firm footing fight to advantage. In these the natives are accustomed to swim and traverse about being immersed as high as their waists, for going naked as to the greater part of their bodies they contemn the mud. To these, indeed, flight was an easy matter and they lay hidden in the thickets and marshes. All which things being adverse to the Romans, served to protract the war."

This description would certainly have fitted the Fylde, but to suggest that Severus had Kate's Pad constructed is just an example of an unscrupulous historian trying to make his guess fit at any price. Herodian was probably referring to Severus' Scottish campaigns. By this time, the Brigantes had little desire left to rebel. True they had done so on several occasions and had inflicted great slaughter on the Romans, but the population of Pilling could not have been sufficiently great to constitute a threat to the Romans.

The Romans were, of course, great road builders, and it is interesting to note in passing, that many of their roads followed the old Celtic tracks, most of which led to Stonehenge. It is very possible they used a track across the sands from Lancaster through Cockerham over Broadfleet River, on to Pilling Lane, Preesall, Hambleton, and crossed the River Wyre at Shard, which they called " Aldwath " or " Aldwith," thence to Kirkham. They constructed a road from Kirkham to Ribchester, and their main road North ran from Preston to Lancaster, passing close to Garstang. Traces of it can be seen near Calder Vale and Scorton.

South of the Wyre, chiefly in the Kirkham area, a few relics of the Roman invasion have been found—battle axes, a broken sword, coins, several cinerary urns, stone hand mills, horse shoe, etc. An iron fibula (brooch) was found, but this might have been Norse. The Rev. W. Thornber says that beneath the peat, in Stalmine moss, was discovered a wine-strainer, made of a kind of pewter ; he says, also, a spear head was found.   But north of the Wyre evidence of the Romans is very meagre.   In the Harris Museum at Preston is a socketed spear head, which was found in Pilling moss.   It is probably of the Romano-British period.   At Hackinsall a bag of coins was found ; some of them are in the Harris Museum. They could have belonged to a British merchant.   They range from Domitian (A.D. 98-117) to Maximinianus (286-305).

Before closing this chapter, there are two other features which might be mentioned.   The first is the " Danes' Pad," the name given to a track which was supposed to have run from the Wyre Peninsula to Kirkham and thence East, and sometimes confused with " Kate's Pad."   It was supposed to have been a broad raised track made of gravel.   The Rev. W. Thornber and John Just described it in great detail, but Mr. J. Burrows, Representative of the Ancient Monument Board, stated that he had actually walked the whole length of the alleged track and nowhere found the slightest resemblance either on or under the ground of a paved road.   If it had existed it had long since vanished.   Mr. G. Milner, late Head Master of Newton-with-Scales School, a very reliable man, who spent many years working on local historical research, said he had found traces of the track in three places.

It seems, therefore, that a track of some kind did exist, but whether it was made by man or was just a glacial deposit will probably never be known.   It is thought by some people to have been pre-Roman, in which case if it did exist, Kate's Pad might have linked up with it and so formed a means of communication with the outside world.   Other people suggest it might even have been of neolithic origin, but if it was such a massive work as Just says, it was most certainly not Neolithic.   Neolithic man did not construct roads.   He was content with tracks.   In any case there would be no need for a raised track in Neolithic times in the Fylde as it would be experiencing dry forest conditions.   The swampy moss conditions did not begin until the Bronze Age.

Finally, the " Portus Setantii " or " Setantiorum "—the " Port of the Setantii."   This controversial subject has been dealt with very fully by others so it can be passed over quickly here. An ancient geographer, Ptolomy, who died about A.D. 151, has left us a map of Britain and on it he had marked " Portus Setantii," which, judging from its name, if it did exist, might have been some- where on the coast of Lancashire.   Some people are of the opinion that it was located in the mouth of the Wyre.   In which case Roman soldiers would have tramped along the shore roads of Pilling to reach it.   But, unfortunately, when members of the Fleetwood and Pilling Historical Societies made two expeditions in August, 1949, to Kings' Carr buoy, where local fishermen say there is a " Roman wall " ; not the slightest trace of any human work was found. There was just an embankment, several hundred yards long, of stones which were of glacial origin. It is simply a " drumlin " and the steep sides are caused by the strong current. Some day the sea may give up its secret, but in the meantime the site of the port is another unsolved mystery.

Devil's footprint - Broadfleet Bridge: legend has it that the Devil was once resident in Cockerham where his malign presence caused widespread failure of crops and livestock. Challenged by the village doctor, parson and schoolmaster to a battle of wits, he was defeated. Furious at being outwitted, he took one stride out of Cockerham to Pilling, leaving his hoofprint on the parapet of the bridge. His next stride carried him to Blackpool where he is said still to live.

CHAPTER 2

Angles, Saxons and Norse

IT is not possible to say exactly when the Romans finally left
Britain. Owing to attacks on Rome by the Goths, Franks, etc.,
they were forced to withdraw troops from Britain to meet the
threats at home. We can assume there would be no Romans left
in Britain by 410 A.D., for in that year the Emperor Honorius
sent letters to the cities in Britain telling them to look to their own
safety. But the Britons themselves were no no means incapable
of self defence. They were able to clear Wales of Irish invaders,
and in 429 A.D., under the leadership of Bishop St. Germanus,
a Frankish Bishop, they put to flight an army of Picts and Saxons
near Mold in Flintshire. But before they went the country was
being attacked from all quarters. In 367 A.D. there was a combined
invasion of Picts, Scots, Angles and Saxons from which the Roman
power never recovered fully.

In 600 A.D. South-Western Scotland, Westmorland, Cumberland and Lancashire composed the kingdom of Strathclyde, peopled
by the Welsh or Brythonic Celts. Pilling was in this kingdom, on
which the Picts, or Painted Men, from Northern Scotland carried
out many raids.

By 684 A.D. the British kingdom of Strathclyde became very
weak and was cut off from Cambria (Wales) and was hemmed in
by the Scots of the North. It became subject to the kingdom of
Northumbria. The people of Northumbria were a mixture of
Angles and Saxons. These people over-ran and took the Southern
portion of Strathclyde. Many British communities in the Fylde
must have survived this Anglo-Saxon invasion, probably owing
to the fact that parts of the Fylde would be marsh or bog and
difficult to reach, but that they had settlements in this district is
proved by the place-names which provide irrefutable evidence.
Names ending in *wick, ham, tun* are English and these are very
common showing that this area, the Fylde, was fairly well settled
before the coming of the Norse. Examples are : Elswick, Bispham
(the home of the Bishop) Kirkham (the place of the Church),
Cockerham (the home on the Cocker), Poulton (the tun or town
on the Pool), Hambleton (Hamela's Town), Singleton, Thistleton,
etc.

Lea is Anglo-Saxon meaning a glade. We come across it in
Winmarleigh—Winmer's glade. Our own Broadfleet is probably
from the Anglo-Saxon " Fleot," an inlet or shallow creek.

The name "Amounderness" may, indeed, date from Saxon

times. Rev. T. D. Whitaker says : "Aimund was an ancient mode of spelling Edmund, and the form of the old Danish genitive case instead of es was er ; Aimunderness, therefore, is the promontory of Aimund or Edmund. Whatever the meaning of the word Amounderness, it is probably of greater antiquity than the name of any wapentake in the country." Pilling is situated in the Hundred of Amounderness. The " Hundred " is the oldest and most interesting of English institutions. It is so ancient that we do not know its origin. It might be a hundred settler families, or a hundred warriors, or the holders of a hundred hides grouped together for the purpose of defence and self-governing. The " Wapentakes " found in several Northern counties, consisted of three " Hundreds " united for the purpose of naval defence against the Norsemen, each Wapentake having to furnish a ship. The meeting places were usually at some conspicuous spot or well-known object. These places were sometimes marked with a cross or stones. At the consecration of the monastery and church of Ripon in the year 705 A.D., amongst other donations of the great Saxon princes and nobles, who were present at the ceremony, were lands near Ribble in *Hasmunderness*, bestowed upon the new foundation. In the next century the entire region of Amounderness was granted by King Athelstan to the Church of York.

*   *   *   *   *

A few dialect words from the Anglo-Saxon still used by the older generation, but fast dying out are :

Aboon—above. A.S. *abufan.*

Ackersprit—potato tubers which grow roots with more tubers at the ends. A.S. *aecer*, a field, and *sprit*, a sprout.

Ess—ash. A.S. *aesce*, ashes. When more peat was burned every grate had a hole under the grate into which the peat ash fell. It is still called the " ess hole."

Attercop—a spider. A.S. *atter-coppa*, a spider.

Back-spittle—a wooden shovel used in baking oatcakes. A.S. *bacan*, to bake.

Boskin—a cattle stall, from A.S. *bos.*

Brat—an apron. A.S. *bratt.*

Deet—daub, dirty.

Dree—long drawn out. A.S. *dreogan*, to endure.

Fain—glad. A.S. *faegen.*

Flay—to frighten. A.S. *fleon*, to flee.

Kist—a chest. A.S. *cist.*

Lark—to play. A.S. *lac*, to play.

Lite—a few. A.S. *lyt.*

Parrock or paddock. A.S. *pearroc*, an enclosure. Compare " Horse Parrock (or Paddock) Lane.

Nesh. A.S. *hnesc*, tender.

Snick-snarl—twisted, such as a rope; or an entanglement.   Eng. *snare.*

Souap—small quantity of liquid.   A.S. *supan*, to sip.

Thrutch.   A.S. *thryccan*, to push or press.

Whang—a shoe lace.   A.S. *thwang*, a thong.

Ullert—an owl.   A.S. *ule.*

*   *   *   *   *

The Saxon bead, which Mrs. M. A. Hargreaves (*nee* Williamson) loaned to the author, may provide the key which may open the door and enable some light to be shed on this period of our story. The bead, which was found when cleaning out the moat, which surrounds the site of the old chapel near Newers Wood, was given to Mrs. Hargreaves' grandfather, Mr. William Hall, at the beginning of the nineteenth century.   It is approximately the size of a shilling .9 ins. by .8 ins.), of a type commonly found in pagan Saxon burials and dates from the middle of the fifth to the middle of the seventh century.   It is made of glass and has a design in yellow enamel encircling it, and was attached to two smaller beads coloured black and blue.   Whilst the finding of the beads in the moat cannot be taken as conclusive proof, when taken into consideration with the fact that part of the foundations of the old chapel (see chapter on The Church in the Middle Ages) resemble those of other Saxon churches, it suggests very strongly the presence of Saxon people on this site.   Moreover, after the onset of the peat and fen conditions, the inhabitants would be driven to the dryer coastal strip. The very fact that the site is sub-circular points to it being the meeting place or moot of the villagers in Saxon times.

If one might venture an opinion, it is very tempting to say that the site of the ancient chapel might be a key site in the story of Pilling and provide a happy hunting ground for future investigators.

What does concern us in Pilling is the coming of the Northmen—the men of Norway and Sweden, sometimes known as " The Vikings."   Vikings means warriors, not men of the viks or creeks, as is generally supposed.   These men commenced their plundering raids about 787 A.D.   In 793 A.D. the old monasteries of Lindisfarne and Jarrow were plundered; in 795 A.D. Scotland, Ireland and Wales ; in 798 A.D. the Isle of Man was over-run. This is important because it was from Ireland and the Isle of Man (850 A.D.) as bases that they invaded England.   They conquered and settled a large part of Northern England.   The colonisation of the low-lying parts of the Fylde does not seem to have been carried out fully by the Norsemen until about 900 A.D., but Norse influence is strong in the whole of the Fylde.

The Hundred of which the Fylde is a part is called " Amounderness."   Dr. Ekwall says : " This is Norse, Agmundarnes,— Agmund'sness (ness—a promontory).   This may be an old name for the Fylde, which forms a headland between the Rivers Ribble and Cocker. If so, Agmundr will have been a Norse chieftain who held the district. He has been identified with Agmund Hold who, according to the Anglo-Saxon Chronicle was killed in 911 A.D. But Amounderness may have referred to a special point or headland, e.g. Rossall Point."

Be this as it may, Scandinavian names are numerous north of the lower Wyre, for example, Stalmine contains " *mynni* "— the mouth of a river (the local pronunciation, " Stawmin " is probably the correct one) ; Rawcliffe is derived from the Norse ; Preesall from " *press* "—a heath, and " *agh* "—a hill (local pronunciation Preesa) ; Hackinsall from " *Hakun's haughr* "— Hakun's mound (local pronunciation Hackinsaw) ; Knot End, a " *knot* "—a shingly headland ; Nateby, the homestead of the neats (oxen) ; Skitham is Norse and Anglo-Saxon ; and Eagland Hill is Norse, " *Eiki lundr*," meaning an oak grove (a lund was a sacred grove where pagan rites were carried out).

The ending " by " is typically Norse.

The place-names show that the Scandinavians who settled in the Fylde were chiefly Norse not Danes, as they were in the east of England. Danish and Norse place-names have certain distinctive features of their own. A Danish test word is " thorpe." There are no " thorpes " in the Fylde.

Norse test words are " breck "—a slope or hill ; " scale "— a hut. Names in " breck " are common in the Fylde.

Within a century and a half after Athelstan's charter, we have another account of the state of the Amounderness. It appears to have been almost completely ravaged by the Norse. It had only three churches, which must have been Preston, Kirkham and St. Michael's, and sixteen villages which were said to be " paucis incoluntur " (few inhabitants). This devastation would probably account for the fact that the Church of York had given up all claim upon the Amounderness, which must therefore have reverted to the Crown. The old claim of the Church was never renewed and William granted this Wapentake to Roger of Poitou in 1094.

The dialect of Pilling shows a very strong Scandinavian influence. Professor Findlay, late of Manchester University, once said : "If a man loses his dialect he loses part of himself." Yet, in his report on 7th June, 1865, Her Majesty's Inspector of Schools wrote : " It is desirable that some effort be made to counteract the broad local dialect." Is it ? It is questionable.

The fact that Pilling was isolated until quite recent times has kept it insular and has meant that much of its language has retained many very old characteristics. Speech has changed very little during the last several hundred years, until recently. Richard Rossall is still spoken of as Richard Rossa, as his namesake was in the Church Registers on the 4th October, 1642, and Curwens are still Corrans as they were three hundred years ago. The fact is Pilling is a little corner of old England and Pilling people should be proud of that fact.

But the introduction of motor cars and motor transport has rapidly influenced speech. Many old words have become obsolete with the passing of the old pre-motor generation.

The following words still used in Pilling but, of course, not confined solely to this district, are of Scandinavian or Danish origin :—

Summat—something. O.N. *sum-hvat.*
Mich—much, Scan. *mycket.*
Backerds—backwards.
Eigh—yes.
Forrud—forwards.
Long sen—long since.
Weel—well.
Sooa—so.
Mun—must, from the Danish *monne.*
Swig—to drink. Danish *swiga.*
Slat—to slop.
Where t'ban ? Danish *buinn.*
Snig—an eel.

Many words connected with the home are of Norse origin, e.g. :
Baking and back board, from *bagebord.*
Dough, from *deig.*
Clap bread, from *klapperkake.*
Tablecloth, from *boardclaith.*
Smoke, from *reeks.*
Thatch, from *thack.*
Blether, from *bladdra.*
A twinter, a two years' old heifer. (Note—Twinter's Head Farm).
A gimmer, a female lamb.
A bull form the Norse *bole.*
Loaf, from *hlaf*, the master of the manor, who provided the food.
Bule, a handle from Danish *boile*, a bent piece. Modern German
  bûgel, a bent piece of wood or metal from which we get our
  modern word bugle, a bent instrument.
Beck, a small stream. Norse, *beckr.*
Scuff, scuft. The nape of the neck. *Skuft* was the withers of a
  horse or more properly the tuft of hair on the neck.
Cap from the Norse *kappè*, a champion. That'll cap him.
Pad from old Danish *pad* and Anglo-Saxon *paad.* Note—
  " Kate's Pad."
Ling is a pure Danish word and old Norse meaning heather. We
  have Ling Row. There must have been, at some time, heather
  in close proximity.
Carr, marshy land. " Carr Lane," which is low lying and liable to
  flood ; also " Jarvis Carr," which was known by that name

more than a hundred years ago.
Wallow, tasteless.
Slack, a hollow between rising land. " Rushy Slack."

Abbreviations are used which are sometimes put down to
speech laziness, but this is not always the case.

One characteristic is the definite article " t," which is an
abbreviation of the old Norse demonstrative pronoun *hit*, e.g.
" He lives down t' road."

Another characteristic is " *i* " for " in," which is pure
Scandinavian, e.g. " It's cold 'i Winter."

It is rather remarkable that the mark of a race of men, the
Norse men, who were dominant in this district for less than two
hundred years, should have endured so long. While it lasted
their domination must have been complete.

**Pilling's two splendid churches: early Georgian simplicity in the 'Old',
opulent Victorian Gothic in the 'New'. Holden's sundial can just be
discerned below the window on the old church. A walk around the
churchyard will quickly reveal the continuity of family names.**

CHAPTER 3

Pilling in the Middle Ages

THERE is no mention of Pilling in the *Domesday Book* (1086). It was probably included in the Parish of Garstang. The surrounding villages of Rawcliffe, Stalmine, Hambleton, Preesall, Nateby, Hackensall, etc., were all mentioned and details of area given.

Garstang is shown as having an area of 28,881 acres and of this less than 1,500 acres were cultivated. Pilling must have been just a few huts in the remaining 27,000 acres of waste, moss and marsh, with a small coastal strip. Communication, apart from one or two tracks across the bog, with the outside world, would be difficult. Indeed, until 1780, the only road was from Cockerham, along the shore and on to Pilling Lane.

The earliest mention of Pilling is contained in a grant from Theobald Walter (later Pincerna or Butler), made between 1194-1199, of which the following is a translation :—

" Know all men present and future that J. T. Walt, for the Divine protection and for the love of the Blessed Mary for the salvation of the soul of King Henry (II) and for the soul of King Richard his son and the soul of John Earl of Moreton (afterwards King John) and of the soul of Randle de Glanvile dear to us and for the salvation of the soul H. (Hubert, his brother, who was Archbishop of Canterbury from 1193 to his death on the 13th July 1205), Archbishop of Canterbury our Brother and of Herveus Walter my father and of Matild' Walter my mother and for the salvation of my soul and of the souls of all my friends and benefactors and ancessors and sucessors, have given and conceded and by this my charter have confirmed all my Haye of Pylin to God and the blessed Mary and the Abbot and Canons of the Premonstratensian order there serving God, in clear and perpetual alms for the building of one abbacy of that order. Wherefore I will and order that the aforesaid abbot and canons there serving God have and hold the said Haye freely, with all its appurtances and the messuages pertaining to it free and quit and absolved from all secular exaction and service from payment of foresters and from all other cause as freely as alms can be given in a free Haye, in wood or plain, in meadow and pasture in waters in pools in fishponds in mills in fisheries in saltpits in marshes both moist and dry and in all liberties and easements of the aforesaid Haye, both those which now are and those which may thence arise.

Witnessed : Will' Poer., Benedict Gernet, Ralph de Bethum,

36

A Piece of a Lancet Window from the Chapel at Newers Wood.

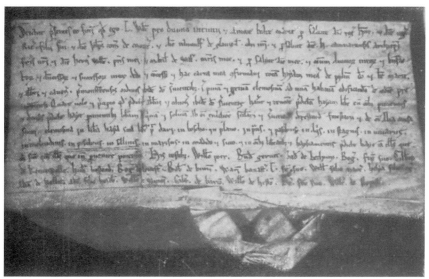

Theobald Walter's Grant of The Hay of Pilling, A.D. 1194-1199. The First
Recorded Mention of Pilling. (Pylin).

Roger his brother, Gilbert de Kentewelle, Hubert bastard, Roger de Leicester, Robert de Brun, Warin Banastre, T. his brother, William the son of Martin, Helias the son of Roger, Adam de Kellet, Adam son of Heseb', William de Winequic (? Winwick), Geoffrey de Barton, William de Heston, Richard his brother, Walter de Slopish (Shrewsbury)."

It is difficult to understand what exactly is meant by " The Abbot and Canons *there*, (i.e. in Pilling) serving God," unless some were living at Pilling.

The Haye (haiae, hay or hey) was a name given to a portion of the forest which was enclosed with a hedge or fence, into which animals were driven, either for capture or slaughter.

Theobald Walter was brother of Hubert, Archbishop of Canterbury. The Honor of Lancaster was forfeited by Count John of Mortain, who later became King John, and King Richard granted the whole of the Wapentake of Amounderness, in which grant Pilling was included, to Theobald Walter in the year 1194 (*Lancs. Pipe Rolls*, p. 81).

The date of the Charter is therefore between 22nd April, 1194, and April-May, 1199, when John was crowned King. This Charter, and others, is (or was) in the possession of Mr. Dalton of Thurnham Hall.

Later, King John deprived Theobald Walter of the greater part of his estate in the Amounderness for wrongfully ejecting Ughtred's son, Richard, from his estate at Broughton and other misdeeds.

Pilling was included in the Royal Forest of Wyresdale. This simply means that Pilling was subject to forest laws, which were very strict, for instance, nobody in Pilling would be allowed to keep a hunting dog or hunt.

On the Monday after Easter Day in the year 1287, Adam de Carlton, Roger the son of Roger of Middle Routheclyve (Rawcliffe) and Richard his brother, were charged at the Lancaster Assizes with having killed three stags in the Moss of Pelyn. T. Baines says : " Were indicted for capturing three wild oxen with the dogs of Richard le Boteller," but this is probably not correct, as the Forest Assizes were to try offences concerning stags not oxen.

Deer were probably not numerous, these three had most likely wandered down from the hills as they sometimes did up to very recent times.

Pilling, on account of its isolation, was necessarily almost self-supporting. The population of a village depended to a large extent on the number of plough teams it could support with which to produce a sufficient amount of bread. At first, this would depend on the monks of Cockersand, but later, after the " Peasants' Revolt " the people began to have more freedom. The Lords of the Manor began to accept rents instead of service, as they found it more convenient, and the villeins began to have their own little homesteads.

In the early days of monastic rule, there is no doubt the majority of the inhabitants of Pilling were almost serfs, bound to the land of the monks. According to the Rev. Dr. Whitaker, the Coucher Book in 1530 gives the names of 350 dependents, which were described as " nativi," but their servitude at that time could hardly have been that of bondmen.

At the time of the *Domesday Book*, and for some time later, the largest measure of land was called a *Carucate*, meaning a team land from the Gaulish *caruca*, a wheeled plough, or the amount of land which a team of eight oxen could maintain in cultivation. This, of course, varied with the type of soil. In heavy stony soil, the amount which the team could cultivate would, of course, be less than on nice light soil. So the area varied. The carucate was divided into eight *Bovates* or *Oxgangs*, which was the amount of land the owner of one ox could maintain. This, again, varied as much as from five to twenty-five acres.

The Lancashire acre appears to have been forty roods in length and four roods in breadth, a rood at that time being twenty feet. The Lancashire acre, therefore, contained 7,111 square yards. The rood in Pilling to-day is still seven yards, known as " Customary Measure." This accounts for the difference in measure to-day in different counties. For instance, a " Cheshire " rood is eight yards. This gives 10,240 square yards in a " Cheshire " or " Big " acre.

The fields were cultivated on a two or three years rotation of crops, and were ploughed in strips with ridges called " Seliones " (from the Anglo-Saxon *seelung*, meaning plough land), to facilitate surface draining. A seillon was not a definite measure, but varied from four to eight to the acre. To-day they are called " lands," but although the practice has ceased of late in Pilling, the older generation can still remember ploughing in four or nine yards " lands." It is a very old custom and the term was often used in deeds, e.g. " Matilda, daughter of Alan of Stalmin, have given all the *seillons* which belong to my oxgang of land upon the butts," 1206-1230. The seillons or lands can still be seen in many of our fields. A point of interest is that they are visible on the land on the seaward side of the shore road at Pilling Bridge, proving that the land there was cultivated at one time and must, therefore, have sunk.

Wages were not big. We are told in the Cockersand Chartulary that, " in the year of our Lord 1272, during hay time, the meadow land at Hulkrigg and Pilling was measured, and there was found to be in the cellarer's meadow 23 acres to mow, in the Susterscale meadow 44 acres, and in Chapel meadow, the Court meadow, and the Moss meadow 31 acres, and note well that when the price for mowing the acre is *threepence*, we shall give for mowing the whole 24s. 6d., when the price is 3½d. the acre for mowing, we shall give

28s. 7d., and when the price is 4d. the acre for mowing, we shall give 32s. 5d. for mowing and no more." 32s. 5d. for mowing 98 acres by hand, with a sickle ! A carter earned from 4s. to 6s. a year with his keep.

Of course, prices were low. A good working horse could be bought for £1 or £2 ; an ox for 10s. ; a sheep for 1s. ; butter was 5½d. a stone. Rents were very low. In the Rental of the Cockersand Abbey for the year 1251, we find William de Pylin paid 6d. and the sum total of the Amounderness was £4 19s. 6½d., but we are not told the acreage.

Since the formation of the peat, timber has been very scarce in the township. In the year 1274 (approx.) John, son of John, the tailor of Kirkland granted to the Abbot of Cockersand that they should wholly take for ever the dead wood in Kirkland. If timber had been plentiful nearer the abbey they would not have gone to the trouble of carting it all the way from Kirkland.

The amount of timber did not increase, for in a Survey of the possessions of Cockersand Abbey in 1536, we are told : " Olde woode of Asshe and Elme within the site of the monasterie and in Pillyn of XI yeres and more by estimation, 1 acre worth XL s."

Again, in a valuation for John Kechyn on 6th June, 1543, we are told : " There be growing about the Scituacion of the seid late Monasterye & graunge and in hedges inclosynge landes apperteynynge to the same schrubbed Okes & Asshes of LX & LXXX yeres growth reserved for Tymber for houseboot (Housebote, wood that a tenant might take to repair his house), ploweboot & cartboot valued at 4d. the tre(e), which is in !ye hole (whole), ...XXXIIIs. (*Cockersand Chartulary*, Chetham, Vol. III, Part III.)

There were, therefore, apart from Cokshot Wood in Ellel, which was about nine acres, 100 trees only, in the whole demesne.

Again, under the same date, we are told, " In Bankhowse & Pyllynge . . . trees growynge abowte the scituacion of the seid tenementes & in hedges inclosynge landes perteynge to the same will barelye suffyce for Tymber to repayr the seid Tenementes and to mayntene the hedges & fences abowte the same . . . . Nil."

The houses were mere hovels, built of the materials that were available, peat or clay and heather mixed, or cobble stones from the shore, or they were of the Cruck type, so called from the Latin *crux*, which means a cross. The gable ends were formed by leaning two tree trunks against each other and crossing at the top. The ridge pole was placed on these. The sides were built up with branches of trees and plastered up with clay. The floors were made of clay, probably covered with rushes.

The only good example of a cruck house remaining to-day is " Moss Houses." Frank Jones' is an example of a house built of peat and Mr. T. Cookson's house at Lazy Hill was built of cobble stones.

Each family occupied a toft or small homestead, with its orchard, garden and paddock, and eked out an existence as best it could, no doubt supplementing its diet by fishing, keeping fowls and making cheese, and netting sea birds on the shore. Vegetables, such as turnips and potatoes were unknown. The main crop was oats, then barley, mainly for brewing the ale and feeding pigs and then wheat ; also some peason (peas and beans). Their bread was probably made of mixed grain, oats and rye called " maslin."

For sweetening they used honey. Many of them kept bees and the majority kept a pig. Taking the local Wills as our source of information, we find the standard of living was low and life was hard. There were few candlesticks, indeed, these would hardly be necessary. It was bed and work. The farm labourer rose at 4 a.m. and worked until 8 p.m. Bed coverings were of canvas and beds of chaff, except in the case of the yeomen farmers who usually owned a four-poster bed with feather bedding. Not until the end of the seventeenth century do we find mention of houses with three rooms, called " bays " and these had only one chimney. If the house had a chimney the testator was usually most careful to mention this fact—also the fire irons.

Many of the people had spinning wheels, winnocks or piggins (milk buckets) and they ate their food off wooden trenchers.

The hinterland of Pilling, stretching from just south of Pilling Water to the River Wyre, was a terrible black morass, which shut in Pilling. It was so awe-inspiring that the monks called it " The Black Lake." It is mentioned in 1190-1212 in a grant of land— " By these bounds . . . . as Swines moor descends into the *Blakelache*, and *Blacklache* into Brock." Lache probably comes from the Norman French " lac," meaning a lake or Saxon " lache," meaning a muddy hole or bog. In 1687, William Stout mentions Heysame (Heysham) Lache.

It is mentioned again in 1268-1284. Liberty was given to the monks " to raise a dyke in a line from the existing dyke at the *Blakelache*." Even in 1536 we are told there were no commons belonging to the Abbey—" But Pyllen Mosse being a foul morass or moor and mete neither for common of pasture nor turbary."

This Black Lake made the people of Pilling a self-reliant, independent, self-supporting, isolated community, with its own craftsmen, blacksmith, saddler, cobbler, wheelwright, etc. They even made their own salt from the sea water and sold it. In fact, it seems to have been quite a flourishing industry. Leland, King Henry VIIIth's historian, in about 1540, said : " At the end of the sandes I saw divers salt cootes wher(e) were divers hepes of sandes of salt strondes, out of the wich, by often weting with water, they pike (this word is still used) oute the saltnes and so the water is drived into a pit, and after *sodde* (sold)."

In a Deed of 1632, Edward Winckeley, *salter*, of Pilling is mentioned. On the night of the 18th and 19th December, 1720, there was an extraordinary flood, when every salt house with great quantities of salt were carried away. In a lease to Richard Tomlinson, dated 5th September, 1767, the Sand Side or *Salt Coot* Field is mentioned. A salt coot or cote was sometimes a furnace where salt was made.

For a fertiliser they dug out the clay from under the peat and spread it on the land. In later days men were paid 1d. each for digging these holes, and so they were called " Penny Holes." A field next to New Hall Farm at Scronkey is called " Penny Holes field," and the holes are still there to be seen. They made fresh land by removing the peat and throwing back the top soil. The peat has been a very important commodity since early times. In a covenant dated 1282-1285, John of Kirkland granted to the monks of Cockersand a road through Kirkland wood to drive their beasts and to fetch and carry their turves (turbis) and from that day to this will be found in most agreements concerning farms and land the right of " turbary," that is, the right to cut and take peat for one's own use.

The waste lands which did not belong to a tun in early times were called " folk lands " and belonged to the people, but later the king, who was considered the guardian, came to regard them as his own personal private property. Moreover, he claimed the Foreshore, the land between high water and low water mark and thus he claimed the Marsh. The King was the Duke of Lancaster and so the Marsh was said to be Duchy property.

The first Duke of Lancaster was Edmund Crouchback, the son of Henry III. He was followed by his son, Thomas, who was beheaded in 1322 for leading an insurrection against Edward II. Then the famous John of Gaunt was made Duke of Lancaster. In 1399 his son, Henry Bolingbroke, became King of England as Henry IV and held the dual titles of " The King, The Duke of Lancaster," which title the King has retained ever since, and by this title he is always toasted in Lancashire and in Lancashire regiments.

In the reign of Henry VIII, war with Scotland, which had been more or less continuous for fifteen hundred years, again broke out openly and the Scots were severely defeated at Flodden in the year 1513. The flower of Scottish chivalry was withered and blasted by the arrows of Lancashire lads, led by the Earl of Stanley, when " Lancashire lads like lions, laid them about," and among the Lancashire lads were Pilling lads we are told in an old ballad :

" From Warton unto Warrington,
From Wigan unto Wyresdale,
From Wedacre to Waddington,
From Ribchester to Rochdale,
From Poulton to Preston, with pikes,
They with Stanley out went forth ;
From Pemberton to Pilling dykes,
To battle billmen bold were bent."

And so here we must leave the men of Pilling practising on a Sunday afternoon, with their bows and arrows, on the marsh by order of King Henry VIII, who forbade the playing of base football on a Sunday.

Road junction at Stake Pool: right to Garstang, left to Lancaster via the sands, and behind the camera to Preesall and Rawcliffe. The house on the right is now the Nat West Bank, on the extreme left the sign of the Elletson Arms can just be seen, while in the background is the smithy. The girl standing in the road, c.1935, would find that much too dangerous a spot in 1997.

CHAPTER 4

Cockersand Abbey

THE story of Pilling in the Middle Ages is closely connected with Cockersand Abbey, so a few notes on it might not be out of place.

In the reign of Henry II, circa 1180-1184, a pious hermit named Hugh de garth, took up his abode at Cockersand. He was held in great respect by the people in the vicinity and was supported by charitable gifts to maintain his hermitage, and later a hospital for the sick and lepers. William de Lancaster II and his wife Hawise granted to him, probably in 1184, " in pure and perpetual alms the place of Askels Cross and Croc (Crook) up to the Pool (Jansen's Pool) together with his fishery in Lune and more beside if they could be made, and all manner of easements in his wood of Wyresdale for the maintenance of a hospital."

In 1186, William de Furness, Lord of Thurnham, granted " to God and St. Mary, and to the Hospital of Cockersand, and to the bretheren serving God there, a portion of his land of Thurnham, to wit, all the land by the Sunken Pool (now Jansen's Pool) which runs down from the moss into the great pool of Crook, etc. . . ."

On the 6th June, 1190, Pope Clement III issued a Bull of Protection and Priveleges to Henry, Prior, of the Hospital of Cockersand. This Bull, which was really the Foundation Charter of the Abbey, said : " . . . We ordain that the regular order, which according to God and the institution of the Premonstratensian bretheren, is known to be founded in that place, shall be inviolably maintained for ever. Moreover, whatsoever possessions and goods the monastery possesses or may acquire . . . . shall remain firm to you . . . . reclaimed patches of land in Wyresdale, all easements (reliefs) within William de Lancaster's wood, etc. . . . land and tithe of mill in Charnock, one oxgang of land in Carlton . . . . four acres of land in Kirkby Lonsdale, twenty-four acres in Hulton Roof, seventeen acres Hilderston, common rights in Yealand, four acres in Beatham, a salt pit in Meathop . . . . two assarts in Cockerham . . . . Moreover, we decree that the liberties and immunities rightly to the said place granted by kings and nobles and especially by William of Lancaster, the founder of your house, etc. . . ."

It will be noticed how its possessions had increased in four years.

In the same year (1190), by the generosity of Theobald Walter, it became an Abbey of Premonstratensian Canons. This change was confirmed by Richard I. This order of "*Pre montre*" originated at Laon in France in A.D. 1119. Its founder, St. Norbert, claimed that the site had been premonstrated or fore-shown in a vision and so called "*Premontre.*" They also took the name, in England, of "The White Canons," on account of their white habits. On the 14th March, 1201, John confirmed the Grant of the site of Cockersand with the appurtenances (Commons, etc.) and "All the pasture of PYLIN to have and to hold in free and perpetual right . . ." This was again confirmed by Henry III on 14th March, 1227.

Soon the Abbot became a power in the land. He was Lord of the Manor in Pilling, and before very long had considerable secular, as well as spiritual influence, in the Fylde and many parts of Lancashire and adjoining counties. He held his Courts in different Manors.

The following extract from a Plea before Hugh de Cressingham, Justice at Lancaster in 1292, is interesting : "The Abbot of Cockersand was summoned to answer to the Lord King by what warrant he claimed to have *weyf, infangenthef and emendation of the assize of bread and ale broken in Pylin, Prestowe (Preesall), Hankenneshow (Hackensall), Stalmyn, Staynoletc . . . . ., Warrington . . . ., Lyverpol, etc. . . .

The Abbot says he does not claim weyf, infangenthef and emendation of the assize of bread and ale broken, but claims to be quit of common fines and amercements of the county and wapentake as is contained in the writ of King John . . . . also King Henry . . . .

The jury say that the Abbot ought not to be, nor used to be quit of common fines and amercements (fines), except only in two carucates of land in Newsum (Newsham) and the Manor of Pylin, and therefore the other lands of the said abbot should remain geldable."

Although the Abbot said he did not claim weyf, etc., it hardly seems likely that the King would have issued a warrant against the Abbot if there had not been some reason for doing so. This would mean the Abbot was claiming powers equal to a Baron.

At Cockerham, a daughter abbey of Leicester, St. Mary de Pratis, had been founded some time about 1153-4 A.D. No doubt, they became jealous at the growing prosperity of their neighbours at Cockersand and disputes began to arise about boundaries, damming up streams and causing floods, trespassing, tithes, etc. However, various agreements were made whereby the monks of

* "Weyf" was the right to take any wandering cattle. "Infangenthef" was the right to hang thieves if taken within the lord's demesne. The important point about this was : Whoever had this right had the greatest power of rule. The emendation of bread and ale referred to the right to control the standard of bread and ale, and fine those who did not maintain the standard.

Cockerham granted to the monks of Cockersand the site on which the hospital was situated, with liberty to build an abbey there, and as a result there was a portion of Pilling across the corner of the Bay at " Bankhouse " or " Bonkhouse " until quite recent times. They also granted two fisheries to be made there or elsewhere and the fish balk they made is still to be seen at Cockersand.

The abbey they built could not, of course, compare in size and grandeur with the greater monasteries, but nevertheless it must have been a fine piece of work, built partly of red sandstone, cut out of the native rock and partly of millstone grit, probably cut and carried from their quarry at Forton. What remains there are, give us some idea of the amount of labour entailed. The thickness of the walls, fit to withstand the terrific Atlantic galès, and one wonders at the quality of the mortar, which has withstood the gales of centuries. The octagonal Chapter House, fortunately, still remains. It is a beautiful piece of architecture. What love and care was bestowed on the exquisite groined roof, supported by an Anglo-Norman column with carved capitals, and resting on a broad plinth of stone. And the sculptured heads on the capitals round the pointed arches—do they represent the heads of the early bretheren ? Around the wall was a low seat of stone. It has been restored by Mr. Dalton and has been used as a family mausoleum for many years.

There is a tunnel, which runs about a dozen feet below ground level for a distance of about sixty yards. It is said to be a drain. It has been cut down from the surface into the solid rock and then built over with sandstone blocks. It is (or was) six feet high. One wonders why so much labour should have been spent on a drain and why it needed to be so deep beneath the surface, or why it needed to be six feet high, when no running water flowed through it. It has been explored, but at the landward end fallen debris has prevented progress. It certainly would have provided a convenient means of escape in the event of the monastery being attacked. It was covered up when the sea wall was repaired in 1952.

In two hundred years the force of the stormy seas began to tell. The sea banks were being worn away. The walls were in danger of falling into the sea, and the canons in desperation, sought help of the Pope, Gregory XI. He granted a relaxation of penance of a year and forty days to penitents who would give alms for the repair of the " monastery of St. Mary, Cockersand, in the diocese of York, situated so near the sea that the walls built for the preservation of its buildings are being worn away and destroyed by the waves." There is still a corner of a wall, perilously near the edge of the cliffs. It is still called " St. John's Chapel " and may be the ruins of a chapel of the Abbey.

St. John the Baptist seems to have been the favourite Saint of the bretheren. They called their little chapel in Newers' Wood by the name of St. John the Baptist. In 1717, the people of Pilling followed with a new one with the same name, and the present church has carried on the tradition. Not many people realise it owes its name to the monks of Cockersand Abbey. Yes, there is much in Pilling to remind us of them.

There is reason to believe the abbot, who was Lord of the Pilling Manor, would not be behind in having the sea-banks built. That the monks were responsible for digging the ditches is quite certain. In a Quitclaim by John, Lord of Stalmine, it says : " in consideration of the sum of twenty shillings, of his rights in the pasture of Preesall and Pilling within the dikes of the said Abbot and granting the said monks liberty to *dig and raise dykes* in a line from the existing dyke at the Blakelake to another dyke belonging to the said monks on the east." This was in 1268-1284.

Again, in a Deed concerning boundaries (see Chapter on Crawley Cross), dated 5th August, 1320, we read : " the Hay (or Hey) of Pylin begins where Pylin (Water) falls into Kocker, ascending Pylin as far as the *made dike* (foveam *factam*), which is called Meredike." Again, " where the cross (Crawley Cross) stands, in a straight line northwards down to the ancient ditch belonging to the said Abbey . . . ."

These ditches are to be seen to-day, still carrying out efficiently the work for which they were made.

It was not all plain sailing for the monks. They had their enemies and no doubt the young bloods from Wyresdale and Lancaster and the Butlers from Rawcliffe would consider them fair game. Indeed, on 31st March, 1234, Pope Gregory found it necessary to write to the English Prelates enjoining them to protect the Convent of Cockersand and to excommunicate all persons committing any act of violence or robbery against the Convent or its servants, who " do occasionally suffer injury and pillage by their aggressors, while hardly is there to be found any who will support them with suitable protection . . . . But our beloved sons . . . . complaining as well of frequent wrongs as of the daily default of justice . . . . You shall with lighted candles strike with the sentence of excommunication those who have profanely seized the possessions, goods, or houses of the aforesaid bretheren . . ."

They did not escape " The Black Death " in 1349. In July, 1363, Pope Urbanus issued a Faculty to Thomas, the Abbot of Croxton, to dispense twelve canons of Croxton and Cockersand, in their twenty-first year to be ordained priests, " there being, on account of the pestilence, but few priests in the monasteries and churches of their order."

No doubt, Pilling felt the heavy hand of the pestilence.

As Lords of the Manor, the Abbots of Cockersand and Cockerham claimed any wrecks which were cast on their shores. In a composition between the two houses in A.D. 1230, the Abbot of Cockersand granted to the Abbot of Cockerham " every wreck which the turbulance of the sea might cast ashore upon the sands of Cocker, or upon lands belonging to the Abbot and Convent of Leicester (Cockerham) . . . *when Divine clemency sent ought.*"

They were good farmers and built a grange where Pilling Hall now stands. It would be quite easy to take their crops by boat across the Bay, and only a couple of miles, much easier than going by Cockerham and Thurnham. They cultivated the coastal strip around Pilling Hall as far East as Crawley Cross and probably as far back as Pilling Water, with isolated spots at Eskham and Skittam, coming westward to the head of Ridgy Pool, across to Union Lane to Head Dyke, and so to the sea.

In spite of this it appears that the Abbey, at any rate in its early existence, was not entirely self-supporting, for in the reign of Henry III, 11th Feb., 1232, safe conduct was given for the Abbot's ship to be sent to Ireland for provisions, and on 16th October, 1382, a Licence was given for the Abbot of Cockersand to import 300 quarters of wheat from Ireland for the maintenance of himself and the convent.

From Cockersand they reached out over the Fylde and founded or served Chapels at Pilling; St. Oswald's, Stalmine; Hambleton, St. Mary's, Singleton; Lund; Poulton, etc. They wielded great spiritual power over the people, as is evident in the Deeds of gifts of land to the Abbey. The donors were most careful to make it clear that the gift was for the health of their souls. And so their work went on until the Dissolution of the Greater Monasteries in 1539. By that time, the Abbey of Cockersand owned lands in Amounderness, Leyland, Blackburn, Yorkshire, Makerfield, Salford, Cheshire, Lonsdale, Kendal, etc.

In " Letters and Papers, Foreign and Domestic, Henry VIII," 1536, the second valuation of the Abbey is given as £282 7s. 7½d. ; bells, lead and goods, £343 18s. 5d. ; religious persons, twenty-two ; servants and others, having living, fifty-seven. The Survey of the Possessions of Cockersand Abbey, A.D. 1536, in the Duchy of Lanc. Rentals and Surveys gives some interesting information on the type of servants maintained at the Abbey and the wages paid. The following are extracts :—

Edwarde Holme, hynde of husbandrie ..	26s. 8d.
George Dyconson, maltemaker	22s.
Leonarde Borow, Carior of (?)	16s. 8d.
John Dobson, Smythe	26s. 8d.
John Ball, Comon Miller ..	26s. 8d.
Richard Hull, tasker of corn	16s. 8d.
Richard Trenchemore, keper of the garners	13s. 4d.
Margarett Kerver and Jenett Herryson, wynowers of corn	16s. 8d.
Rauff Higham, wright for the Abbey ..	33s. 3d.
Robert Brade, ploughe driver .. food and clothes.	
William Bell, horse keper	26s. 8d.

The following is a list of stock, and their valuation, at the Abbey in 1536, probably including that at their Grange at Pilling :—

4 Quarters of wheat at 33s. 3d. the quarter ..	£4 13s. 3d.
4 ,, ,, oat malt at 15s. the quarter ..	60s.
4 ,, ,, barley at 20s. the quarter ..	£4 0s. 0d.
4 Waynes (carts) 3s. 12 yokes 12d. & 12 cheynes of Irone 4s.	8s.
3 Coulters & 3 Shares at	20d.
2 harrowes with Irone tynes	2s.
9 yong Spenynges (pigs)	6s. 8d.
1 olde Hogge	2s. 6d.
1 olde bore, 2s. 8d. ; 2 yong bores, 2s. ; & 5 sowes, 8s.	22s. 8d.
53 mylche Kyen at 8s. ye pece	£23 3s. 0d.
30 Hekforthes (heifers) of 3 years olde at 6s. 8d. the pece	£10 0s. 0d.
42 Stirkes of one yere olde at 3s. 3d. the pece ..	£7 0s. 0d.
3 Bulles at 7s. ye pece	21s.
2 Mares & one Fole at	20s.
2 Coltes of 2 yeres olde	23s. 4d.
1 colte of one yere olde at	3s. 3d.
3 olde Hores to carye loodes	10s.
28 Ewes & 28 Lambes at 20d. the cople ..	45s.
17 wilde Kyen at 6s. ye pece & one caulff ..	102s.
24 draught Oxen at 30s. the yoke	£18 0s. 0d.

The land and meadows in Pilling occupied by the Abbot were valued at £26 10s. 8d. rental. That occupied by tenants was rented at 69s. 3d.

There were nine tenants:—

John Richerdson	3s. 4d.
Richard Johnson	10s. 0d.
Christofer Thorneton ..	3s. 4d.
The wife of Thomas Holme ..	13s. 4d.
John Bell	10s.
John Lacas	3s. 4d.
William Patryk	2s.
William Holme	14s.
Philip Thorneton	10s.

The grange or pasture called Le Pyllyn, in the Parish of Garstang, with all manner of commons, was estimated to contain 1,000 acres.

On the 28th March, 1539, the King demised to John Burnell and Robert Gardner, for £73 6s. 8d. the farm of the site of the late monastery with the demesne lands, the grange called Pillyng and the lands belonging, with the rectory of Garstang.

On the first day of September, 1543, King Henry VIII conveyed to John Kechyn, who was the King's receiver and a farmer at Cockersand, for £700 8s. 6d. all the site of Cockersand Abbey, with appurtenances, including the Grange called Pyllyn.

John Kechyn went to reside at Pilling Hall.

So passed a great institution and with its passing left Pilling without a spiritual shepherd for some time.

John Kechyn does not seem to have been interested in maintaining the monastic buildings—perhaps he leaned to Protestantism. The Abbey was systematically pulled to pieces and taken away. It served as a quarry for anybody wanting stone. The farm buildings in the vicinity to this day bear witness of this, and no doubt Pilling has had its share in the shape of grave stones, gate stoops, bridges, building material and perhaps the " plague stones " on the shore came from Cockersand.

The Chapter House still keeps guard as it looks out across the Bay, a silent sentinel. How long it will continue to do so will depend on those who value old things.

See " The Chartulary of Cockersand Abbey," Chetham Society.

CHAPTER 5

Crawley Cross

ONE result of the Norman Conquest was a tremendous growth in religious fervour and the power of the Church. Religion pervaded the lives of the people. The Pope became more powerful than Kings and Emperors. The Cross was omnipotent and its sanctity inviolable. With a cross in his hand a Priest could halt a rebellious horde or face an insurrection. Under the shadow of the Cross men would die happily. A bargain made under the Market Cross was absolutely binding. A pursued man could be sure of sanctuary if he could reach a cross, even if pursued by the most bloodthirsty ruffians.

So it is not surprising to find a large number of crosses in Lancashire, especially in the Amounderness, where, excluding Preston, there are more than seventy crosses of one kind or another.

They can be classified as follows :—
1. Preaching.
2. Churchyard.
3. Roadside.
4. Market.
5. Sanctuary.
6. The Cross at cross roads.
7. Boundary.

Their names tell their own story.

They are to be found more thickly grouped where the influence of the Abbeys of Cockersand and Cockerham was greatest. The Editor of the *Chartulary of Cockersand Abbey* writes : " The register speaks eloquently of the sentimental piety of the Lancashire people in the thirteenth century, but an examination of the registers of religious houses in the country leads to the conclusion that the feeling which induced so many people dwelling in West Lancashire to have regard to the ' health of their own souls and the souls of their ancestors and successors' was comparatively absent among the inhabitants of the eastern half of the county." Most of the possessions of the Abbey were obtained as gifts. The bargain being that in return for the land the monks would look after the spiritual welfare of the donor, who was most particular to ensure that a clause safeguarding his soul and that of his relations should be included in the Deed of Gift. (See Theobald Walter's Deed of Gift, chapter 3.)

Once the monks had the land they took very good care to ensure there were no loopholes whereby they might be deprived of it. Boundaries were very carefully designated, and this is un-

Crawley Cross.

[Photo by H. Curwen.

The Stones on the Shore.

[Photo by H. Curwen.

doubtedly the reason why the monks went to the trouble of erecting Boundary Crosses ; especially is this the case with Cockersand Abbey, which had a jealous neighbour at Cockerham. There are several references to crosses in the Chartulary. In 1190-1212, in a Grant from Ughtred, we find, " as Swines moor descends into the Blakelache, and Blacklache into Brock, enclosing the said land as far as the oak tree *marked with the cross*, as the crosses and marks define the same."

Again, in A.D. 1230, in a Composition between Peter, Abbot of Ouston and Hereward, Abbot of Cockersand, we read : " And as to the division . . . . it ought to remain as formerly appointed between them, to wit from the cross set up where the three bramble bushes were."

As it was marked with a cross the boundary would be inviolable.

Crawley Cross was one of these Boundary Crosses. It marks an angle in the boundary line between the Hundreds of Lonsdale and Amounderness and is at the junction of the three parishes of Pilling, Cockerham and Winmarleigh. It is a plain cross, 16 ins. high and 12 ins. in width, cut out of millstone grit. The cross is socketted into a modern stone pillar about 3 ft. 6 ins. in height. It is invisible until one is quite close as it stands in a dike. The following extracts from the Cockersand Chartulary have an interesting bearing on its history : " The bounds of the demesne of the Hey of Pilling begin where Pilling (Water) falls into Coker, ascending Pilling (Water) to a certain made dike, called Meredike, following that dike as far as it goes, thence in a straight line southward and eastward to a point opposite *Crowlache* (Crawley Head), from thence in a straight line unto Crawley Head, following Crawley unto Pilling Water again . . . . ."

The date of this Deed is 5th August, 1320. Therefore, Crawley Cross was standing there before then.

Another reading as given in the Chartulary (Vol. I, Part I, page 48) is : " Ascending the same to the head and from the head of Pilling Water in a straight line by the Hedge (or Hey) between Scytholm (Skittam) and the south, unto the head of the West Pool (now Ridgy Pool) down the same unto the White Reap (Union Lane where Out Rawcliffe, Stalmine and Pilling township boundaries meet) following the White Reap westward to Farther Beckhead, descending Farther Beck into Lune, ascending Lune unto where Coker falls into Lune and thence ascending Coker unto the place first named to wit where Pilling Water falls into Coker."

The Abbots of Cockerham and Cockersand mutually agreed that the following boundary should for ever be maintained, " to wit, commencing at Crawley Head, *where the cross stands*, in a straight line northwards down to the ancient ditch belonging to the said Abbey towards Pilling (Water), following the same as it turns into Pilling Water, and so by Pilling Water along the ancient course into the sea."

The cross still stands, in a bleak, desolate spot. The monks have gone, but it remains there, a mute, faithful guardian of its masters' demesne ; a silent, lonely witness of their thoroughness and tenacity ; unnoted and forsaken by all but the birds, whose cries have enlivened its dreary solitude through hundreds of years. Little did the men who put it there realise that we should gaze on it six centuries later.

Guard it well, posterity !

Pilling Mill: picture taken between the wars by which time it was no longer in use. The chimney in the background is on the corn drying kiln. Note the bonnet worn by the lady. Such headgear was still to be seen in the district after World War II.

CHAPTER 6

The Plague in Pilling

ON the shore may be seen two large stones. There is a story that a ship was wrecked on the sands and some sailors managed to get ashore and were received into a cottage. The sailors had the plague and the inhabitants of the cottage caught it and all died and were buried there. This story is most improbable.

On the 15th November, 1947, members of the Pilling Historical Society lifted these stones and on one could be seen indistinctly the following inscription carved in relief :

C DICK
ONSON
MAR
GRET
HIS
WIFE
BURID
OF JU
16

Obviously " WIFE " could not refer to a sailor.

Hewitson, in his book, *Our Country Churches and Chapels*, written in 1872, when the inscription would be less worn and more easily decipherable, says the date was either 1650 or 1660.

1650 is probably correct. Pilling was suffering terribly from the plague in July, 1650.

No, the most probable story is that the Dickonson family lost father and mother and the children brought the stones across the sands from the ruins of Cockersand Abbey to mark the spot where they had buried their beloved parents. To corroborate this theory, Dickonsons were living at the " Ridge " in 1636 ; also there was a Richard Diconson, yeoman, living at Preesall in 1627 and it is not beyond the realms of possibility that the people could have been buried on the shore instead of in the church yard. The death roll was terrific and the Curate, the Rev. John Lumley, might not have been able to cope with all the burials. It was not unusual for people to be buried in unconsecrated ground. There is said to be a " plague pit " in the old chapel yard in Newers Wood and to substantiate this Mr. P. Ritson, who assisted in the excavations, carried out by members of the Fylde Historical and Antiquarian Society in 1936, on the site of the old Chapel, stated they " came across thirteen skeletons in *one* cutting."

There were, of course, many plagues which visited England during the ages, and they had a very great effect on our history as the number of deaths was so great that a great scarcity of labour was caused, resulting in Acts of Parliament being passed to prevent men leaving their villages to seek more remunerative work in other parishes. Also, it resulted in the enclosures, more sheep breeding, etc. But we are only concerned, here, with the epidemic which did such awful execution in this district in the early seventeenth century.

Mr. R. Sharpe-France, County Archivist for Lancashire, in his book, *The Plague in Lancashire*, tells us that this plague was of two main types known as the " Bubonic " and the " Pneumonic " (lungs). The bubonic was the more common and less severe, having a mortality of something over 60 per cent, whereas the pneumonic had a mortality of almost 100 per cent. The plague was carried by rats and was passed from one animal to another not by direct contact, but by fleas. These charming little creatures sucked up the plague bacilli (*Pasteurilla pestis*) with the blood. When the rats died the fleas sought other pastures—man !

Of the two kinds of rats, the Black rat and the Brown rat, the Black rat was more usually plague infected, and was very common in the seventeenth century, whereas now it is very uncommon.

The period of incubation of the bubonic disease was about six days. It appeared very suddenly, with fever and headache. The face became haggard and the eyes sunken and bloodshot. A great thirst developed and the tongue swelled and cracked. By the second or third day swellings called " buboes " appeared. These burst and discharged an evil smelling pus. The sufferer usually died within a week.

The pneumonic affected the lungs and the patient soon died. It was very contagious and could be passed without the agency of fleas.

There were many favourite medicines—filed horses' hooves, crabs' eyes, and the black points of crabs' claws. If the patient became delirious it was recommended that his head be wrapped in the lungs of a sheep.

Many causes were given for the plague. Earthquakes, the weather, comets, eclipses, gluttony, drunkenness. But the chief cause of the spread of the disease was unsanitary conditions. Until quite recently, the floors of the cottages were made simply of clay, covered with rushes, in which all kinds of filth accumulated.

Unfortunately, the Register of Burials for Pilling does not commence until 1685, and so we do not know how many people died. However, figures are available for some of the surrounding villages and these are interesting, and may throw some light on conditions in Pilling. The following are taken from the respective Registers of Burials :—

Year	Stalmine	Garstang	Cockerham
1614	.. 10	41	56
1615	.. 12	49	68
1616	.. 7	75	36
1617	.. 5	163	63
1618	.. 15	38	57
1619	.. 13	70	45
1620	.. 18	89	44
1621	.. 16	84	72
1622	.. 30	84	108
1623	.. 11	6	265
1624	.. 12	Blank	43
1625	.. 13	2 (?)	48
1626	.. 18	74	40
1627	.. 23		42
1628	.. 11		40
1629	.. 15	26	44
1630	.. 17	30	51
1631	.. 10	53	51
1632	.. 19	50 (May-June)	39
1633	.. 31	44	36
1634	.. 22	63	57
1635	.. 22	81	35
1636	.. 27	60	28
1637	.. 19	68	58
1638	.. 18	79	62
1639	.. 21	67	53
1640	.. 16	38	65
1641	.. No further	—	68
1642	.. record	—	52
1643	..	—	67
1644	..	—	63
1645	..	21	53
1646	..	46	48
1647	..	38	39
1648	..	63	61
1649	..	89	66
1650	..	124	76

Stalmine must have had a terrible time in 1623. There were 11 burials registered and then the following distressing note : " There was buried the tyme that I were sick fortie and above or thereabouts at the parochiall Church at Stallmin within the year above written." It appears that the Parish Clerk was struck down with the Plague but was fortunate to recover, and it might be that the same applied to Garstang, as the Register is blank for most of 1623-1625.

Garstang suffered badly again in 1632. During May and

June, fifty people were buried, mostly women and children, and the Township was exempted from supporting other parishes as it had to maintain its own poor, " beeing about the number of a hundred att the least." The number of burials at Garstang seems high but it might be as well to point out that people from the surrounding districts, as far as from Bilsborrow, were buried there. It seems to have had another visitation in 1650.

Cockerham suffered very severely in 1622 and 1623, and Out Rawcliffe, we are told, was infected with the Plague in 1633.

So we see that Pilling was almost encircled for thirty years by parishes literally steeped in plague germs. In proportion to its size and population, this area suffered worse than London in the " Great Plague " of 1665, but it is not recorded in the History books !

Pilling, perhaps protected by its defences the sea and the Moss, staved off the attacks until 1650—at least we have no records until then. In the Lancashire County Records Office there are three very interesting documents. Two of them, letters, bear the signature of the Rev. John Lumley, the first Curate of Pilling of whom there is any definite record, and who was " silenced for severall misdemeanors." The other, an Order from the Quarter Sessions.

They tell a remarkable story and are quoted at length as follows :—

1. (QSP. 34/10) A Request for Relief for the poor people of Pilling.
The sixt day of July 1650

These are humbly to entreat your worships to be pleased to take notice that we the Inhabitantes of Pilling whose names are here subscribed seinge our Town is visited with the plague (as is supposed) do desire an answerable competence for the subsistence of so many poore families as are noe way able to subsiste without the reliefe of our neighboring Townships, Soe humbly prayeng for your worships health and happines we rest

The number of the poore in Pillinge as we have counted 260 and upwardes

> John Lumley cler
> Richard Johnes
> William Bell
> James Bradshawe
> Lawrance Garner
> Thomas Johnes

2. (QSP. 34/11) An Order from the Quarter Sessions.
At the Sessions of the Peace held at Preston
in Amounderness, 11th day of July, 1650.

These are (according to the direction of the statute of I James chapter 31) to certify this Court, That at the suit and request of the Inhabitantes of Pilling, upon Saturday last wee

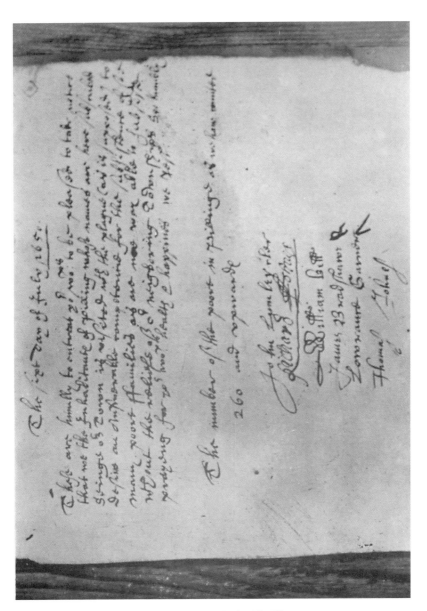

Petition for assistance during The Plague.

did graunt an Assessment of one Fifteene within the Parish of Garstang (which doth amount unto the summe of £8 19s. according to the Booke of Rates for the releefe of the Poore infected in Pilling, The number of the Poore is certified to bee above 260 under the handes of John Lumley, Clearke, Richard Johnes, William Bell, James Bradshaw, Lawrence Garner, Thomas Jones. And since they doe sollicite to have the same enlarged and continued weekelie for the better keeping of theire poore within themselves.

> Tho. Whittingham
> Jirehjah Aspinwall

3. (QSP. 34/12)   A further Request for Relief.

It seems that either the Petitioners had had a recount or the numbers of sick had risen rapidly between the sixth and tenth of July.

May it please your worships to be informed that we whose names are hereunto affixed being inhabitants of Pilling do certify your worships according to your discretion that there are 300 and upwards and not able to subsist without relieffe and what your pleasures are to dispense what somes of money for their provision for one month's time—we conceive that twentie pounds a week will but only serve them for breade and what your worships think meete for other provision we refer it to your discretion humbly craving to an Assessment with all expedition for we are att this present at greate want thus with our humble duties we humbly take our leave and rest.

> Your humble servants
> Jo Lumley Clerk
> Richard Johnes
> William Bell
> Richard Johnes Younger
> Richard Whytsyd

Pilling the Xth of July
1650

The " Fifteen " granted was not sufficient, so the Assessment was raised to thirty-five pounds sixteen shillings within the Parish of Garstang. A " Fifteen " was a form of local rate in medieval times. It was a fifteenth of a man's income for a year and was a basis for local taxation.

From this it appears that Pilling was in a sorry state. At least one in two, or three, was suffering from the plague. Little wonder if they did not all find resting places in the Chapel yard.

But this was not the end. The next year we are told that the relief for the Townships of Pilling, Cabus, Forton and Holleth and for the repayment of those who helped in the relief—taking food, seeing that the people remained in their own parishes or shooting dogs or cats—was not sufficient by £50.

And so it dragged on until 1652, when we find the last mention of plague in Pilling. In fact, with the exception of a few minor outbursts, it disappeared from this country.

Mr. Sharpe-France thinks the main reasons for its disappearance were, better sanitary conditions and better type of houses and the coming of the brown rat which drove out the black rat—that arch carrier and spreader of plague.

So even if the stones on the shore do not mark the burial place of any of our forebears, they do remind us of the terrible time through which they went in this, the most tragic chapter in the story of Pilling, and for this reason, do let us see they are treated with respect and some reverence.

May they rest in peace.

Funeral cortege at Stake Pool in the early 20ᵗʰ century. The building in the foreground, now a bank, was evidently still a private house. In the background is St. William's R. C. Church, completed in 1893.

CHAPTER 7

The Church in The Middle Ages

THE story of the Church in early times is shrouded in mystery. The shape and contour of the site of the old Chapel near Newers Wood might point to a Saxon christian structure having been there in very early times. This is supported by the finding of the Saxon beads in the surrounding moat, also the font in use at present at Eagland Hill is almost certainly a Holy Water Stoup of the Saxon period and the Rev. J. D. Banister stated that it had been taken from this Chapel. The establishment of the English Church can be said to date from Saxon times and many were built where the villagers used to hold their moots or meetings. These sites were, very understandably, on mounds and were often surrounded by moats. The early churchyards were usually circular and later became rectangular under Norman influence.

It is a well-known fact that it was often the practice to build a church on the site of one of an earlier period.

In May and June of 1952 members of the Pilling Historical Society excavated the site of the old Chapel, which is situated on an elliptical piece of ground one hundred yards by sixty, surrounded by willow trees and a moat some eighteen feet wide ; a beautiful secluded spot, far from the madding crowd.

Very little of the original foundations remain. The stones were undoubtedly used for the foundations of the 1717 church and those not used for that purpose were probably taken and used on neighbouring farms, as the grave stones were. But there was quite sufficient material remaining to build up a fairly accurate picture.

The whole of the site was covered with eighteen inches of rubble, composed of thick slates, mortar, sandstone and plaster. The plaster clearly showing brush marks pointed to the interior being plastered. Beneath the rubble were patches of a coarse yellow sand of some two inches in thickness and forming either the floor of the chapel or a bed for flagstones or tiles.

The foundations of the north and south walls were fairly complete, and enabled the outside width of the chapel to be ascertained as 19 ft. 6 ins. The west wall could not be traced. At the west end of the south foundations was a flag stone and several sandstone blocks which might have formed the floor of a porch. At the north-east corner was found a pile of sandstone blocks, two feet high, and the base three feet by three feet three inches.

The top stone (now supporting the altar stone), 2 ft. 3½ ins. by 1 ft. 5½ ins. by 6 ins., was chamferred on two sides and chiselled for

An Artist's Impression of the Chapel at Newers Wood.—*By W. Cardwell.*

ornamentation. The whole had been mortared together. They probably formed the base of a buttress at the north-east corner, but why these stones had been left in situ is a mystery. Perhaps they had been regarded with special sanctity—perhaps the altar steps.

The Altar Stone of The OLD Chapel.

Part of the east wall was found. This determined the length as 28 ft., overall measurement, excluding the porch (?) portion. The south-east corner was interesting as it was built largely of boulder stones and was definitely round. This is a characteristic of Saxon churches. The apses or eastern ends were round. The south wall and south-west corner also contained many boulders. This portion was very similar to the walling of other Saxon churches. The chapel, which ran due east and west, was built of red sandstone, probably brought from Cockersand, and had twin lancet windows. The altar stone, which is in a good state of preservation, measures 6 ft. 8 ins. by 3 ft. 8 ins. by 7 ins. It is pre-reformation and still clearly shows an incised cross at each corner. In the centre is a rectangular depression, which probably contained the relics. Further excavation of the site of the chapel yard might provide incontrovertible evidence of a Saxon place of worship.

It does seem quite certain that there was a religious building of some kind in Newer's Wood in the reign of King John. There is evidence to support this, for Theobald Walter's Deed of Gift of the Haye of Pilling says quite clearly, " have given all my Haye

of Pilling to . . . . the Abbot and Canons . . . . *there serving
God.*" "*There*" was, of course, Pilling, and the inference must be
that they must have had a building in which to serve God.

T. Baines, in his *History of Lancashire* (Vol II, page 537, sec.
Edn.) states that a chapel here is named in a Charter of Robert
Fitz Bernard to the Hospital of St. John of Jerusalem, in the time
of King John. When the Rev. J. C. F. Hood, vicar of Garstang,
was in London searching for records of St. Thomas' Church, it
is said he discovered several references to the first Pilling Church
which showed clearly that it existed in the twelfth century.

The monks of Cockersand built a grange at Pilling Hall very
shortly after the foundation of the Abbey and the Chapel was
probably attached to it, not on the same spot, but near Newer's
Wood, for in the year 1217, Pope Honorius granted to the Canons
of Cockersand a privilege for the quiet and seclusion of their
Granges, these buildings being declared equal in sanctity to Churches
(*Hist. of Richmond*, Vol. II).

On the 20th November, 1493, William, Bishop of Lichfield,
granted a Licence to a devout nun, named Agnes Bothe *alias*
Schepard, who desired to leave the Priory of the Blessed Mary at
Norton to lead a solitary life in a cell near the chapel of Pilling in
the parish of Garstang. (*Chetham Miscellanies*, Vol. III). In
the Rental of Cockersand (1501) appears the following entry :
" Md yat Annes Schepte hasse payn to James ye Abbott of Coker-
sand for her lyving-iis iid to me and vis viiid to ye Convent."

As mentioned in a previous chapter, the favourite saint of the
monks was St. John the Baptist, and so this chapel was dedicated
to that saint. It was served by a monk from Cockersand and was
used by the inhabitants. On Saxton's map, 1577, St. John's
Chapel is shown a little distance from Pilling Hall.

On the dissolution of Cockersand Abbey by Henry VIII in
1539, the chapel was left deserted for a time, but in Queen Elizabeth's
reign, services were again held, and the Curate in charge had an
allowance of £10 made to him. Apparently, in 1621, Sir Robert
Bindloss, who was impropriator (an impropriator is a layman who
holds lands of the church or an ecclesiastical living) by the Rectory
of Garstang took the tithes from Pilling, which, by the way, were
worth £42, a considerable sum for those days, was withholding his
share towards the stipend for a curate at Pilling.

Accordingly the following order was made by the King, James I.
" An order upon a Reference from ye Kinge touchinge ye tithes
of Pillyn in the County of Lancaster and findinge of a Curate there.
Whereas it pleased the Kinges most excellent Majesty upon a
petition preferred to his Highness by Thomas Jones on the behalfe
of himself and 60 other inhabitants of Pillyn, within the Rectory
of Garstange, in the Countie of Lancaster, against Sr Robert
Bindlosse, Kt., proprietor of the said Rectory of Garstange, for
withdrawing the meanes and not mainteyninge a Curate att Pillyn

chappell, within the said parish and for exactinge of Tythe of the inhabitants of Pillyn wch they ought not to pay, with other informacons of vexation, extertion, and oppressions therein conteined, to referr the consideracon thereof unto us. Whereupon wee have examined and fully heard the same debated before us deliberated, and doe thinke fitt that a competent means be raised for the maintenaunce of a minister or curat of Pillyn, with the consent of the said Sir Robert Bindelosse and Richard Weetmore, gent, authorised for the peticoners by writinge under their handes as agreed to be as followeth. First that from henceforth there shall bee a minister from time to time continually kept att the said chappell of Pillyn, to read and say divine service upon all Sundays and upon all holydays appointed by the Church of England and to doe the other rites and dutyes belonginge to the divine worpp and service of God used and allowed in the said chappell in the late Queene Elizabeth her tyme And that towards the maintenance of the said m'ster for the tyme being, and the XL[s] heretofore allowed out of or parcell of the XL[li] rent paiable to the Kinges mat[ie] his heires and sucessors for the said Rectorie of Garstange, shal bee yearly payd to the said m'ster att the audit att Lancaster as hath beene accustomed by his Ma[ties] receiver there, and because the same funde of XL[s] only will in no sorte mainteyne a minister, the said Sr Robert Bindlosse out of his charitable devocon and att our instance and request, albeit it seemeth unto us that hee is not thereunto compellable by lawe, is contented and doth freely consent and graunt for him and his heyres to give and pay yearly, forever, for the further and better maintenance of the said m'ster the yearly fonde or payment of tenn pounds to be paid halfe yearly out of the Tithes of Pillyn, within the said Rectory of Garstange viz at Whitsuntide and Martymas . . . . and whereas itt appeareth unto us that the ffarmer of the demesnes of Pillyn, who heretofore gave lodginge and dye[tt] to the m'ster there, as also the rest of the Inhabitants within Pillyn who are to receive spirituall comfort thereby, should likewise contribute to this soe pious worke, we do think fit that the Inhabitants, other than the ffarmer, shall pay . . . the yearly summe of eight pounds . . . . and for that it is mete that the ffarmer of ye dem[ns] there having the best parte of the landes in Pillyn . . . . doe paye yearly for ever vi[l] xiiij[s] iiij[d] towards the further maintenance of the said minister."

November 30 1621

G. Cant. Geo Coluert.*

The church Registers do not commence until 1630 but it seems that from that time to the present, the incumbency has never been vacant for any considerable length of time.

* From Archbp. Abbot's Register, Vol. III, Lambeth Palace Library and Chetham Publications, " History of Garstang," Fishwick.

In 1650, the Parliamentary Commissioners reported that at " the chappell of Pillin there is noe minister but the Cure supplied by Mr. Lumley who hath been silenced for severall misdemeanors, the Inhabitants being very many humbly desire they may be made a Parish, and that a minister and competent maintenance bee allowed."† The Parish could not have been without a Curate very long.

The population must have been considerable, as we know that on 10th July, 1650, there were 300 suffering from the plague and if this were, say, a half of the total it would mean a population of at least 600. One wonders how this number managed to get into the tiny chapel and in 1716 we are told that the number had increased to " above one hundred and forty families."

The position had become so serious that a Petition, headed by the Rev. John Anyon, the Incumbent, supported by a large number of parishioners, was sent to the Bishop of Chester praying that a new chapel might be built in the centre of the Township. A copy of this Petition is among the church papers and is quoted fairly fully as follows :

" Whereas upon the humble petition of John Anyon, Clerk, Robert Bennet, William Smith, William Hall, and John Threlfall minister and Chapel Wardens of the Chapelry of Pilling in the County of Lancaster lately presented to the Right Reverend Father in God, Francis, Lord Bishop of Chester, on the behalf of themselves and the several inhabitants freeholders and charterers of and within the said chapelry that is to say Roger Hesketh of Northmeals in the said County Esq. Robert Hesketh gent. son and heir apparent of the said Roger Hesketh, Edmund Hornby Esq., John Addison, William Bell, Richard Dickinson (?) sen, Mary Thornton widow, Stephen Ribby, Thomas Bell senr, Agnes Bell widow, Ellen Kirkham, William Shepherd, Richard Tomlinson, Thomas Bell jun, Richard Dickinson jun, John Mount, John Fox, Thomas Jollys, John Hey, Thomas Escam, William Mason, Margaret Porter, James Tomlinson, sen, Anne Shepherd, Joseph Gardner, Henry Lea, Jennet Threlfall widow, Thomas Townson, Mary Danson, John Noare, Jane Bond widow, George Thompson, John Jackson, James Tomlinson jun, William Clark, Jennet Bibby widow, Richard Jones, William Bibby, Abraham Smith, James Procter, Henry Smith, Philip Tompson, Margaret Hey, Robert Smithson, Henry Piccop, Elizabeth Williamson, Richard Clark, Thomas Tayler, Elizabeth Burton, and William Williamson, showing and setting forth that at the time of the erecting and building of the present chapel in Pilling aforesaid (which is very ancient), there were but seven houses besides the Mannor house in the said chapelry. That the said Chapel was originally built in the east part and confines of the Chapelry near

† Chetham Publications, " History of Garstang " and " Notitia Cestriensis," Vol. 2.

to the Mannor house, for the conveniency of the Lords and owners
of the Mannor and Lands whereof the Chapelry consists and that
the said Chapelry, being then increased to above one hundred
and forty families, and the inhabitants thereof become very numerous
the present Chapel was not near sufficient to contain them, but
there was an absolute necessity for the same to be enlarged, or a
new one to be built in lieu thereof, and that as well the Lords and
owners thereof (save some few who either lived out of the said
Chapelry or were in such circumstances as not to contribute either
to the Church or poor) were desirous and had agreed to have a
new chapel built (without any charge or trouble to any that did
or should oppose so pious a work) in the middle or centre of the
apelrsd Chy (where the landlords were willing to give a convenient
piece of ground for a chapel yard) most of ye Inhabitants living
on the west side of the sd Chapel, and there being very few families
on the East part of the sd chapelry and the said petioners praying
that they might have his Lordships leave and order to erect a new
Chapel intended to be twenty two yards in length and seven yards
in breadth between the walls and that they might make use of the
materials of or belonging to the present old Chapel for that purpose,
and that the chapel yard of the present old Chapel might forever be
appropriated and secured to and for the use of the Minister for
the time being of the intended new Chapel, and the said Lord Bishop
having considered the said petition was pleased to give his licence
or faculty for the building of a new Chapel and converting and
making use of the timber and materials of the old one, provided his
Lordship had sufficient security given him for the making and
perfecting of a new Chapel. Now know all men by these presents
that the said Roger Hesketh etc. . . . do hereby for securing the
erection and building of the said new Chapel for the better satisfaction of the said Lord Bishop, for themselves, their heirs, etc.,
covenant, promise, grant and agree that they or some of them
will before the end of fourteen months next, wthout any charge
or trouble to any person or persons that have or may be against
ye building of such new Chapel (other than such sumes of money
which they shall voluntarily give), erect and build, or cause to be
erected and built, in good sufficient, decent and workmanlike
manner, a new Chapel, to be such length and breadth as before
menconed, in or near the middle or centre of the said chapelry,
to be for ever after ye erecting and building thereof repaired and
maintained at ye charge of all the Inhabitants, Freeholders and
Charterers of and within ye sd Chapelry, etc. . . . . and the sd
Roger Hesketh and Robt Hesketh do hereby, for themselves, their
Heirs etc. . . . covenant and promise to the said Lord Bishop,
his successors that ye said chapel yard belonging to ye present old
chapel as the site or ground whereon the said chapel now standeth,
shall for ever hereafter be appropriated, goe and remain to and for
the sole proper use, benefit and behalf of ye Minister for ye time

being of ye said intended new Chapel etc. . . . and ye said Edmund
Hornby doth agree, for himself, his heirs etc., that ye old Chapel
yard as ye scite whereon ye same chapel now stands shall for ever
be appropriated for the sole use of the Minister etc. . . . For the
true performance whereof the said Roger Hesketh etc. . . do
hereby bind ymselves, their heirs etc. . . to the said Bishop in the
sum of three hundred pounds etc. As witness their hands and
seals ye third day of October in ye year of our Lord 1716."

That was the death knell of the old Chapel. It was pulled
down and all that remains now are a few stones in the buildings of
Pilling Hall Farm ; a piece of a lancet window ; the grass covered
foundations and a grave stone with the inscription :—

> Richard son
> of Christop^r
> Clark of this
> Town was bu
> ried here
> Feby ye Xth
> 1720

THOUGHTS IN AN OLD CHURCH YARD

Now come with me to Newers Wood,
And stand with me where monks have stood.
In this old spot so still and green
Come, you will see what I have seen.

Look in the dark and dismal past
When light begins to shine at last,
And men of God come from afar ;
At least seven hundred years there are.

See Father Abbot and his men,
" Here must we build to God again
A chapelry though small and low
To which on Sabbaths they can go."

And so across the Bay they row,
In boats so small and ladened low
With stones from Forton, Cockersand,
With heaving breath their loads they land.

And then with loving hands they build
A chapel soon with people filled,
And so Christ's work they carry on,
For us to do when they are gone.

C

We here in Pilling owe them much.
Their dikes still show the experts' touch.
As with great skill the Moss they drained,
While spiritual welfare they maintained.

And now the monks have all gone by.
To see them go we heave a sigh.
We shall not see their like again.
Such godly and industrious men.

Next when the Plague struck rich and poor
I then can see them weeping sore.
And holes they dug both wide and deep,
Where loved ones could for ever sleep.

Yes.   Parson good and brave I see.
Thy name remembered, John Lumley.
Although thy fate we know not what,
We trust that Heaven will be thy lot.

" Too small ! Too small !" was next the cry.
Another church both broad and high,
On the west side we must build
With our own men both strong and skilled.

And so the wood and stones they take,
To help them their new church to make.
" Too small ! Too small !" Again they'll cry.
We'll build a bigger to God on high.

'Tis meet we leave this hallowed spot,
With lingering memories we have got.
Richard, son of Christopher Clark,
Long since dead but left his mark.

CHAPTER 8

The " Old Church "

THE " Old Church," as it is known, bears the date on the Key Stone, 1717. It was consecrated in 1721. The Incumbent at the time was the Rev. John Anyon. It is said to be one of the finest examples of a Georgian Church in existence.

Life during the next hundred years seems to have moved along fairly evenly. The people had their recreations, they kept their holidays, they looked forward to " The Feast " every year. In 1754, 5/- was paid " To Mr. Coulton at Pilling Feast." The Church went from strength to strength and soon the cry " Too small " was again heard. The Chapel would not hold all the God-fearing people of Pilling. In 1813, a Faculty was granted to raise the roof and build a gallery. The Curate at that time was the Rev. James Potter. Many unflattering stories have been told about him but nevertheless he filled the church to overflowing. What methods he used we do not know.

The following extract from a Conveyance of a Seat in the new Gallery is both interesting and informative. There are several copies in existence :—

" This Indenture made the Twentieth day of June in the year of our Lord Christ one thousand eight hundred and sixteen between The Reverend James Potter the Incumbent Minister of the Chapel of Pilling in the County of Lancaster, Robert Whiteside . . . . and Thomas Bagot . . . . late Chapel wardens of the same Chapel and . . . . Inhabitant. . . . Whereas a Faculty or Licence under the seal of George Markham Master of Arts, Commissary of the Archdeaconry of Richmond in the Diocese of Chester and bearing date on or about the eighth day of June one thousand eight hundred and thirteen was duly decreed and granted to the said Reverend James Potter, Robert Whiteside, Thomas Bagot, with full licence and authority to remove and take away the then old roof of the said Chapel and also to raise the walls of the said Chapel one yard and six inches in height to substitute and place thereon another roof entirely new and well ceiled and plaistered and covered with the Westmorland or Lancashire new slate and further to erect and build a Gallery at the West end and North side of the said Chapel capable of containing seventeen Pews or slope Seats each of Seats or Pews to contain in length nine feet and in breadth three feet and to sell and dispose of such Seats or Pews when so erected by Public Auction to such of the Inhabitants and Parishioners of the said Chapelry as stand in need thereof. The Monies to arise from such

[Photo by F. J. Gornall.

The Old Church, Interior.

[Photo by F. J. Gornall.

The 1717 Church.

Sale or Disposition to be applied in dischargeing the expenses incurred by making the said alterations and improvements . . . and whereas the said James Potter, Robert Whiteside, Thomas Bagot have proceeded in and finished the said Buildings and Seats and on the nineteenth Day of October one thousand eight hundred and fourteen, they also proceeded to sell the said Seats by Public Auction in pursuance of Advertisements previously issued for that purpose . . . ."

(Signed) James Potter, Robert Whiteside, Thomas Bagot, Wm. Hall.

The following is a list of the items of Costs :—

		£	s.	d.
1814. To John Lambert as per Contract for Gallery and Roof		304	0	0
Do. Extra expenses on the Roof		24	7	7
To Mr. Dowbiggin for Faculty		10	3	4
5th March. Richard Carter, glazing ..		12	7	0
Blacksmith		5	12	4
Clark's wages and work		5	15	0
To John Corless			6	6
19th Oct. Auctioneer for selling seats in Gallery		1	1	0
To Interest for £100 borrowed ..		5	0	0
Richard Carter, glazing			4	0
Wm. Shrigley for painting		23	0	0
Clark's wages and work..		6	1	8
John Corless' Bill			16	0
Blacksmith		1	15	8
Antony High for Plaistery dressing front of the Chapel etc.		9	6	0

Even after the extension there was a great difficulty in finding accommodation for the worshippers. In the Vestry Minute Book is an entry on 8th November, 1861 : " It was agreed that the Sunday School Scholars should be kept in the School during Morning Service at Church to afford more room for adults at this service."

In 1861 the original chapel yard burial ground, which only extended up to the present path on the West side, running North and South, had become full.

The Rev. J. D. Banister, in a letter to Henry Gardner, Esq., says : " The old yard is so full of graves that it is desirable to have the new ground consecrated as soon as may be. I have just talked over the subject with Mr. R. C. Gardner and Mr. Corless and they strongly recommend that an equitable price should be paid you for the land by the Township."

In a minute, dated 5th May, 1862, it says : " It was proposed by Mr. James Bourne and seconded by Mr. Corless that the amount of compensation to Messrs. Gardners for the Land added to the old Burial Ground at Pilling should be at the rate of one hundred and fifty pounds per customary acre." (7 yds. 1 rood).

Again, on 24th September, 1862, it was unanimously agreed " that a rate of fourpence halfpenny in the pound be laid on all rateable property in Pilling for defraying the charges for the additional Burial Ground to the old Chapel Yard, and the expenses of the Conveyance thereof, and also for the payment of the consecration charges of the new ground."

There is a Draft copy of the Conveyance among the Church papers, but the price to be paid is left blank, so we do not know the actual amount paid, but on a letter from Rev. J. D. Banister to Henry Gardner, Esq., dated 23rd June, 1859, is a pencilled note " Cost about £200." This would appear to be rather over-estimated as the area is given as 3,812 sq. yards. It is therefore quite definite the land was bought from Messrs. Gardner and paid for out of the Church Rate.

The sentence of Consecration was granted on 25th August, 1862, when the Bishop visited the district, and says : " That for the purpose of enlarging the said Burial Ground a certain piece of land has been purchased from the Reverend John Gardner of Skelton Parsonage near Redcar in the County of York, Clerk L.L.D., and Henry Gardner of Sion hill near Garstang and conveyed to our Petitioner the said James Dawson Banister by a certain Conveyance bearing date the twenty-sixth day of July one thousand eight hundred and sixtytwo."

The church yard was again enlarged in 1887. The Deed of Consecration, dated 24th June, 1887, says : " Whereas it hath been represented unto Us James, by Divine Permission, Lord Bishop of Manchester by a Petition on behalf of the Reverend John Wilson Waithman, Clerk M.A. Incumbent of the Parochial Chapelry and Church of Pilling in the County of Lancaster within our Diocese of Manchester, William Shepherd and Richard Kay, Church Wardens, and the Reverend Thomas Philips, Clerk M.A. Curate of the Chapelry and Church of Pilling, That in order to provide accommodation for the burial of the dead of the Parochial Chapelry of Pilling an additional Plot of land containing Two thousand one hundred and seventeen yards immediately adjoining the present Churchyard of Pilling has been purchased from the Reverend John Gardner L.L.D. late of Skelton in the County of York, since deceased, for a sum of fifty pounds. That the said Plot of land was conveyed . . . . by Deed dated the twenty second day of September One thousand eight hundred and eighty four as an additional Church or Chapel yard or Burial Ground for Pilling."

And so,
> " Beneath those rugged elms, that yew tree's shade,
> Where heaves the turf in many a mouldering heap,
> Each in his narrow cell for ever laid,
> The rude forefathers of the hamlet sleep."

Yes, there they lie, Spiritual Pastors, faithful School Masters, hard-working yeomen, loving wives and mothers, all have played their part. Their tomb stones keep their memory fresh.

One in particularly arrests our attention, that
" Sacred to the memory of Sarah, wife of William Sandham, who departed this life 27th July, 1800, aged 70 years. She was the mother of 12 children, four of which she had at one birth and they lived three weeks."

These quadruplets were christened on 29th March, 1765. Their names were Ann, John, William, and Alice. John and Alice died on 9th April ; William, 14th April, and Ann 15th April.

In spite of difficult conditions, the people seemed to enjoy more than the allotted span of life. The longest-lived person of whom there is a record was Joseph Gregson, who died on 11th January, 1803, aged 99 years.

Again the cry " Too small " was heard.

The new church was built and the old one was no longer required. The closing Services in the Old Church were held on Sunday, 19th June, 1887. The preacher in the morning was the Rev. T. Philips, Curate in charge, and in the afternoon the Rev. E. D. Banister, Vicar of Whitechapel, Goosnargh, who had acted as Curate for some years for his father, the Rev. J. D. Banister. The church was crowded, upwards of four hundred being present. The children were sent home to make room for the adults. Although the Rev. E. D. Banister had left the Parish eleven years previously, it was evident by the large congregation present that they still held him in great esteem and affection.

He took his text from Jerimiah vi, 16.

The old church almost suffered the same fate as the old chapel at Newers Wood.

At a sitting of the Manchester Consistory Court, before Chancellor Christie at the Diocesan Registry Office, " The Rev. J. Wilson Waithman, incumbent of St. John the Baptist's, Pilling and Messrs. W. Shepherd and R. Kay, Churchwardens, applied for a faculty to remove all ornaments, brasses, or monumental inscriptions, from the present old church to the new church, when completed, as nearly as possible in the same position, and to pull down the old church, except such portions as it may be thought desirable to retain as a mortuary chapel, or as a building in which to keep such relics of the old church as it shall be considered advisable to preserve, and other necessary implements and articles used in the church. The right of the pew holders will be protected."

The Faculty was granted on 26th May, 1887, but fortunately, the old church has not been pulled down.

The Lords of the Manor have the privilege of nominating a Clerk in Holy Orders to the Bishop of the Diocese to be presented to the living. In an Indenture, dated 9th December, 1833, between the Lords of the Manor of Pilling for regulating the nomination to the Chapelry thereof, it was agreed between Edmund Hornby, John Gardner and Daniel Elletson that, " Whereas Edmund Hornby did nominate the Rev. J. D. Banister to the perpetual curacy of Pilling, the said John Gardner, his heirs shall be entitled to the next nomination then Daniel Elletson and so on in succession."

Stake Pool Post-Office and general store: an informal group taken around the time of the Great War. Run by the Moon family, the store provided not only groceries and hardware, but also, as may be seen on the leading cart, a variety of farming requisites.

CHAPTER 9

The New Church of St. John the Baptist

ON the 28th February, 1883, a Public Meeting was held in the National School room for the purpose of taking into consideration the erection of a new parish church. The Vicar, the Rev. J. W. Waithman, M.A., after some preliminary remarks, moved the following resolution, which was seconded by Mr. W. Shepherd, Churchwarden, and unanimously agreed to, viz : " That in the opinion of this meeting, the time has now come when it is desirable to make an effort to raise the necessary funds for the erection of a new Parish Church." A letter from the Rev. James Cardwell Gardner, Vicar of Butler's Marston, Worcester, was then read, in which he promised to give the sum of five hundred pounds to the building fund, " As a thank offering to Almighty God for the great mercies to his departed parents,"—the late R. C. Gardner Esq. and Mrs. Gardner, of Fluke Hall, subject to certain conditions as to the site of the proposed church. (The site desired by the Rev. J. C. Gardner was where the ' Golden Ball ' Hotel now stands.) Mr. T. Corless of " Springfield House " moved the following resolution, which was seconded by Mr. J. Cross and unanimously agreed to, viz : " That this meeting desires that a hearty vote of thanks be accorded to the Rev. James Cardwell Gardner for his most generous offer of five hundred pounds, and gratefully accepts the same, always subject to the conditions contained in his letter, and also subject to the necessary consents being obtained."

The Vicar then announced that, including Mr. Gardner's offer he had received promises of assistance amounting to £2,650.

Messrs. T. Corless, W. Shepherd, Richard Kay (Church Wardens), Andrew Kay, Joseph Gornall and William Jackson were appointed members of the Committee, with power to add. Mr. Corless was appointed Treasurer, and the Rev. J. W. Waithman was appointed Chairman and Secretary.

The next meeting was held on the 7th March, when it was decided :—

1. That Messrs. Paley and Austin, Architects, of Lancaster, be asked to furnish plans for the new church.
2. That a box be placed in the porch of the old church, to receive the freewill offerings of the people towards the erection of the proposed new church.
3. That no effort be made on the part of the Committee to raise funds from the parish of Pilling until after Easter.
4. That none of the farmers be asked to do the carting by way of gift in lieu of a subscription.

[Photo by F. J. Gornall.

St. John the Baptist's Church.

The Vicarage.

On 21st March, 1883, Mr. Austin inspected the proposed site in the company of Rev. J. W. Waithman, Messrs. Corless, Nutter and Gornall.

The following copy of a letter from Mr. J. Nutter is interesting :

Croft House,
Burton,
Carnforth.
22nd March, 1883.

My Dear Sir,

I saw Mr. and Mrs. Hornby this morning to whom I named what I suggested, and I am glad to say Mr. Hornby will become surety for £4,000 and he desired me to say so, so that anxiety will be removed from your mind. They are very pleased that the plans will be put in hand at once and Mrs. Hornby feels anxious to see them. She hopes the elevation will be substantial and good. She hopes a Tower may be built and completed along with the body of the church. You must push the Architects and get them to put the plans in hand at once, as it is most desirable that the work should be begun early this summer, so as to get as much as possible done before winter sets in.

Yours faithfully,
J. Nutter.

At a meeting of the Building Committee held on Friday, 14th September, the following resolutions were agreed to :—

1. The " Reserved Space " in the church yard is insufficient for the erection of the new church and is consequently condemned by them.
2. That in the event of the Rev. J. Cardwell Gardner's Site being rejected by the Parish, the new church be built in a field commonly known as the " Ship Meadow " (the present Church Field), subject to the necessary consents being obtained.
3. That the Wardens be instructed to go round and take the opinion of the Parish respecting the above sites, by ballot.
4. That every parishioner, male or female, of the age of twenty-one years and upwards be entitled to vote.
5. That the Poll take place on the 22nd, 23rd, 24th, 25th, 26th and 27th October, 1883.

The Ballot seems to have been carried out very fairly. One hundred posters and one thousand Ballot papers were ordered. The result of the Poll was : For Rev. J. C. Gardner's site 137 ; for the Ship Meadow site 251.

For some reason the church was not built on this site either.

At the next meeting, held on 1st February, it was decided the church should be built in a field situated between the School and Mr. T. Alty's house, called " Barn Field," and belonging to the Rev. Dr. Gardner, one of the Lords of the Manor and Rector of Skelton-in-Cleveland in Yorkshire, subject to the necessary consent being given.

The Vicar expressed himself very strongly in favour of the proposed site and read a letter from Dr. Gardner, in which he stated he " would willingly give for a site any land he had that the Parish would like " for a site for the new church.

This was accepted and at the next meeting, held on 8th July, it was decided : " That a walk be made connecting the church yard with the site of the new church, situated in a field belonging to the Rev. Dr. Gardner, thereby prese ving unbroken the link uniting God's Acre with the House of God." From this it would appear that the responsibility for maintaining this path is the Parochial Church Council's. Although I am not aware of the path being actually dedicated to the Church by Dr. Gardner, it must have been made with his knowledge and consent. It was also agreed that compensation be paid to Mr. Alty for half-an-acre at the rate of £12 per acre.

The Vicar seems to have been ill for some time and unable to act as Chairman, but returned to this duty on 1st February. Mr. Corless was appointed Vice-Chairman.

On 28th May, 1884, Mr. Nutter called on the Vicar and stated that Mrs. Hornby and Major Hornby would each give £250 to make good the sum lost by the rejection of the site desired by Rev. J. C. Gardner, who finally withdrew his offer of £500 in an interview on 27th March, 1884. It seems his desire for his site was in deference to a wish expressed by his father, Mr. R. C. Gardner.

On 16th June, 1884, the Plans and Specifications were received from the Architects, Messrs. Paley and Austin, and on the 14th July the tenders were accepted. Contracts were signed at a meeting held on 3rd October, 1884. At the same meeting, the Vicar announced that Mr. William Dilworth, the foreman of the masons had offered to do the carved work on the font for the new church as a gift to the Parish, provided the Committee would find the stone. The offer was accepted and Messrs. Paley and Austin promised to furnish a design for the font so as to ensure its being in harmony with the general character of the sacred Edifice.

The next point to be decided was who should lay the Foundation Stone. It seems to have been impossible to arrive at a definite decision, so it was decided that the Stone should be laid by the Committee without having any public ceremony.

Then the following memorandum appears in the Minute Book : " The Foundation Stone of the New Church of St. John the Baptist, Pilling, was laid on Friday, May 22nd, 1885, at 3 p.m., in the presence of the Rev. J. W. Waithman (Chairman), Messrs. William Shepherd, Richard Kay, Andrew Kay, and William Jackson, by

Thomas Corless, Esq.

Springfield House, Pilling.

(Signed) J. W. Waithman, M.A.

Vicar of Piling."

The First Surplice Choir in The Parish Church, 1896.

J. Parkinson, T. Shepherd, F. Hall, D. Ellwood, T. Hall.
J. Hall, (Sexton), T. Dickinson (Organist), Rev. R. T. Gardner, Rev. J. C. Gardner, J. Kay, R. Bradshaw, E. Ritson.
F. Danson, G. Gardner, O. Hall, R. Kirkby, W. Morley, R. Shepherd, J. Kirkby.
R. Hall, T. Hodgson, R. Bimson, T. Rossall, J. Porter.

On the 25th February, 1886, Mr. Paley, in consequence of "absurd and grossly exaggerated reports regarding alleged sinking of the foundations of the New Church, came over and made a thorough examination of the cracks." Nevertheless, in spite of the reports being "absurd and grossly exaggerated," at a meeting held on 8th October, 1886, it was decided that Mr. W. Harrison's tender for taking down and making good the portion of the West end of the North aisle that had suffered from the slight settlement of the Tower, should be accepted by the Committee. The amount of the tender was £22 10s. 0d.

The Rev. J. W. Waithman was forced to resign the office of Chairman on 6th April, owing to ill health, and did not resume office until 13th February, 1888. The curate in charge, Rev. Thos. Phillips, took over the office until 6th July, 1887, when for some reason he resigned, his place being taken by Mr. T. Corless until Rev. J. W. Waithman resumed office.

The following is a copy of the Contractor's Account :—

	£	s.	d.	£	s.	d.
Wm. Harrison (Mason)	4,601	16	8			
Timothy Hird (Carpenter)	946	10	0			
Walmesley & Co. (Plumber) ..	308	8	6			
T. Cross & Sons	191	10	0			
John Grundy	63	0	0			
H. T. Miles	6	2	6			
T. Hird, Communion Table ..	37	0	0			
J. B. Hartley, Porch Gate ..	9	1	0			
	6,163	8	8	6,163	8	8
Architects	339	9	6			
Clerk of Works (Mr. T. Mawson)	117	11	4½			
	457	0	10½	457	0	10½
Stone for Font and carriage ..	1	17	5			
T. Hall, Furniture	5	7	8			
Wm. Singer, Frame for Pulpit ..	2	13	0			
	9	18	1	9	18	1
Jackson & Parkinson, Surveyors ..	2	2	0			
Manstead & Gibson	11	3	7			
Fees on Consecration	10	4	4			
Bishop's Secretary	1	11	6			
	25	1	5	25	1	5

SUNDRIES—

Cheque Book and Ackerman ..	1	19	2
Rev. J. W. Waithman, Stationery	2	8	9
Robt. Alty, Compensation for Field	6	0	0
Jas Collinson, Rails, etc.	8	5	5
Thos. Hall, Railing and Gate ..	2	10	0
do. Rail, wood and work	2	5	0
Swarbrick, Plumbing	1	0	1
Jos. Preston		14	6

25 2 11   25 2 11

Total   .. £6,680 11 11

LIST OF DONATIONS

	£	s.	d.
The Lord Bishop of Manchester	50	0	0
Rev. Dr. Gardner, Skelton Rectory ..	500	0	0
Major Hornby, Dalton Hall	1,200	0	0
Mrs. Hornby	200	0	0
The Late Mr. R. C. Gardner, Liverpool	100	0	0
Miss Gardner, Liverpool	100	0	0
Mr. Benjamin B. Gardner, Liverpool ..	100	0	0
Mrs. T. Gardner, London	100	0	0
Mr. T. Little, Liverpool	100	0	0
Mr. C. T. Clark	100	0	0
Mr. Frank Gill, Manchester	100	0	0
Mr. T. Corless, Pilling	100	0	0
Mrs. Corless	100	0	0
Miss Corless	60	0	0
Miss A. Corless	60	0	0
Mr. W. B. Corless .. .. .. · ..	60	0	0
Mr. T. Corless, Junr.	60	0	0
Mr. J. D. Corless	60	0	0
Capt. Bird, Crookhey	250	0	0
Mrs. Titley, Barwell Rectory	50	0	0
Mr. T. Harrison, Fulwood Park, Liverpool	100	0	0
Mr. E. H. Harrison, Liscard	50	0	0
Mr. W. Bennett, Heysham Tower, Lancaster	5	0	0
Mr. J. Nutter, Croft House, Burton ..	10	0	0
Miss Baldwin, Green Ayre, Lancaster ..	20	0	0
Mrs. Peebles	5	0	0
Mr. J. S. Gardner and Family	110	0	0
Mr. P. Candlish	10	10	0
Mr. R. Preston Gill, Ashton-upon-Mersey	100	0	0
Miss Gill, Manchester	50	0	0
Rev. J. W. Waithman's Relatives ..	100	0	0

Mr. James Sykes, Liverpool	.. ..	50	0	0
Canon and Mrs. Ware ..	.. ..	5	0	0
Collected by the Committee	.. ..	150	12	0
Mrs. Verdin, Liverpool ..	.. ..	5	0	0
Miss Banister	.. ..	5	0	0
Mr. T. Nicholson	.. ..	5	0	0
Interest at Lancaster Bank	.. ..	41	17	5
Mrs. Rice	.. ..	5	0	0
Miss Gardner	.. ..	50	0	0
Mr. Robert Bradley.. ..	.. ..	5	0	0
Mrs. Bourne, Huddersfield..	.. ..	5	0	0
Mr. T. Dobson, Windermere	.. ..	5	5	0
Mrs. James Bradley, Forton	.. ..	5	0	0
Miss Baldwin	.. ..	5	0	0
Miss Gardner	.. ..	50	0	0
Mr. J. Thornton, Walton, Liverpool	..	1	0	0
The Misses Elletson, Ambleside ..	..	2,000	0	0
Jas. Williamson, M.P., Lancaster..	..	25	0	0
Mr. Jas. Pratt	.. ..	5	0	0
Mr. Cuthbert Danson ..	.. ..		10	0
Offertories, Tea Parties, etc.	.. ..	272	17	11

£6,707 12 4

Some Interesting Items of Expenditure

	£	s.	d.
To Henry Cross (Blacksmith) Stakepool, 30 picks sharpened			7½
do. 14 score 16 chisels sharpened at 5d. score		6	1
„ Mills and Morgan, carving altar table and railing	4	10	0
„ Joseph Preston, Fleetwood, numbering seats ..		14	6
„ Jones and Willis, Birmingham, 200 flax hassocks*	5	12	0
do. 83 brass umbrella holders	14	10	6
„ 1 Brass Alms Dish	3	10	0
„ R. S. Newall, Liverpool, copper wire Lightning conductor and fixing	16	7	0
„ Jonathan Collinson, Garstang, 97 Socket pipes	2	4	5
do. 2 carts at 3/4 day each		6	8

The Sentence of Consecration of the new Church was granted and carried out by Dr. Moorhouse, Bishop of Manchester on 24th June, 1887. In the Sentence it stated : " That a new church had been erected and built by voluntary subscription in accordance with plans prepared by Messrs. Paley and Austin of Lancaster, Architects, upon a Plot of land containing Two thousand nine

* In April, 1950, £42.10.0 was paid for 120 blue hessian hassocks.

hundred and forty one square yards (part of a close called 'Barn Field') situate near the site of the said old church and churchyard of Pilling which plot of land was given for that purpose by the Reverend John Gardner, L.L.D., late of Skelton in the County of York, Clerk in Holy Orders, now deceased and by him conveyed to the Ecclestical Commissioners for England and their successors under the Church Building Acts."

So the great work of the Rev. John Wilson Waithman was brought to fruition. The new Church makes a fitting memorial to him.

The first meeting in the Vestry was held on Monday, 7th November, 1887. It was convened to arrange about building a wall on the South side of the church. The tender of Mr. J. Collinson & Sons was accepted, viz : " To build the new wall, provide all materials for building the wall including carting and labour, for the sum of eleven shillings and six pence per lineal yard." There is no record of the cost of this wall but next year there is an item " Boundary walls and gates to J. Collinson & Sons, £137 7s. 0d." The first gates were made of wood.

On 14th December, 1887, the Vicar and Church Wardens, Wm. Shepherd and Richard Kay opened an account with the Lancaster Bank, to be known as " Parish Church Organ Fund," a cheque for £25 being a donation from Miss Jennet E. Gardner, being deposited.

Mr. Thomas Corless (Senior) saw the church consecrated but died soon after (21st Jan., 1888).

On the 13th February, the following Resolution was passed at the Vestry Meeting : " That this Committee desires to place on record their sense of the great loss which they have sustained by the death of Mr. Corless, who from the first had held the arduous post of Secretary of the new Parish Church Building Fund Committee, and also for a considerable period acted as Vice-Chairman to the above Committee." The Rev. J. W. Waithman was instructed to write to Mrs. Corless informing her of the Resolution, at the same time expressing on behalf of the Committee their deep sympathy with herself and her family in the irreparable loss which they had sustained.

The West window, by Meyer & Co. of London and Munich, was installed by his widow and children to his memory.

The East window, designed by Messrs. Burleson of London, was the gift of the Misses Elletson of Parrox Hall to the memory of the Rev. Dr. Gardner. The small West window is of St. Margaret, by Shrigley and Hunt of Lancaster, and is to the memory of Melita Godfrey, the daughter of Mrs. Pearson by her first husband and was the gift of the Rev. T. Pearson and Mrs. Pearson. At a Vestry Meeting held on 10th April, 1901, the Vicar, the Rev. T. Pearson, drew attention to the need of a new organ for the Parish Church. The organ used at that time was an American organ presented by Miss Corless and Mr. Williamson in 1894. It was decided to start a fund to be entitled " The Banister Memorial Organ Fund," and a Committee was appointed. The organ was built specially by Ainscough of Preston and was subscribed to by the Lords of the Manor, and the parishioners, and in this respect the name of Mr. Joseph Cross should be particularly mentioned. The cost was £400. It was dedicated on the 24th February, 1903. The brass inscription plate was given by Mr. J. Cross, who lived in Lancaster Road.

Mr. J. Cross also presented the church with new wrought iron gates in 1912.   Also, when he died, he left to the Vicar and Church Wardens £100 3 per cent Debenture Stock of Lancs. and Yorkshire Ry. Co.   The interest to be used " To keep in good repair and order his family grave and subject thereto shall apply the dividends for the benefit of the deserving poor residing in this Parish."

The " new " chancel lamps were presented by the Rev. T. Pearson and friends and cost £10 10s. 0d.

The hymn boards, first used on Easter Day, 1906, were the gift of Christopher and Margaret Atkinson (sister of Mrs. Pearson).

The B-flat bell was given by Mr. and Mrs. S. Kellet of Brick House, in memory of their daughter Alice, and the large tenor bell was given by Dr. S. A. Nield-Faulkner in memory of his mother.

The jewelled cross on the altar was bequeathed by Mr. B. B. Gardner in memory of his parents.

The Memorial Cross in the churchyard was erected in memory of those men of this Parish who fell in the First World War, 1914-1918.

The base stone was laid by Rev. T. Pearson, M.A., on 4th February, 1920, at 10 a.m.   The Dedication, by the Venerable Archdeacon Hornby took place at 3 p.m. on Sunday afternoon, 29th February, 1920. It was designed by Austin and Paley of Lancaster and was executed by Mr. Thomas of Lancaster.

The costs were :—

Messrs. Austin and Paley ..	£25	0 0
Mr. Thomas	£208	0 0
Labour	£25	0 0
Total ..	£258	0 0

The Reredos was erected as a thank offering for the safe return of those who served in the First World War from this Parish and also as a thank offering for the peace.

The costs were :—

James Hatch & Sons, Lancaster	£388	0 0
Austin and Paley	£380	0 0
	£768	0 0

It was dedicated by the Rev. T. Pearson at Morning Service on Christmas Day, 1920.

The Episcopal chair was given by Mrs. R. Kellet, in memory of her husband, the late Richard Kellet, J.P., Church Warden from 1927 to 1949. It was dedicated at Morning Service on the 4th February, 1951, by Rev. R. A. Kennedy.

The beautifully carved Prayer desk was made by the Rev. R. F. Cookson, vicar of Barton, and presented by him and his brother, Mr. E. Cookson, both natives of Pilling, in memory of their parents. It was dedicated by Rev. F. M. Cubbon on Sunday, the 9th December, 1951.

The fish weather vane has a significance. The fish was an early christian symbol and the Greek word for fish—" Ichthus "—was a secret " pass word."

Taking the letters separately, we have :—

I   IESOUS—JESUS.
CH   CHRISTOS—CHRIST.
TH   THEOU—GOD.
U   UIOUS—SON.
S   SOTER—SAVIOUR.

Jesus Christ the Son of God the Saviour.

Before closing this chapter, another fact might be mentioned. For quite a considerable time the Incumbent's salary had been augmented by a rate known as " The Minister's Salary Rate." This was usually ½d. in the £, but at a Vestry Meeting held on 29th March, 1894, at the earnest solicitation of the Vicar, Rev. R. T. Gardner, it was decided that the annual rate known as the " Parson's Salary " should no longer be levied, but that following an old custom, all the offerings on Easter Day, both in the Pilling church and at St. Mark's, Eagland Hill, should be given as an Easter offering to the Clergy.

A summer scene in Pilling Village before the Great War: the women and children on the left are local, while the more formally dressed ladies in the road are evidently Blackpool holiday makers who have come by landau or wagonette on a day excursion to Pilling.

Ling Row cottages were demolished around the beginning of World War II, but Bodkin Hall in the background is still standing. The name, Ling, having the meaning of heathland, was a term used in Lancashire to denote the moss.

LING ROW PILLING

A carefully posed group in front of Moss Cottages around 1900. The houses are of 'cruck' construction, that is: the gable ends are built around two long curved timbers reaching from ground to ridge, upon which the roof framework is supported.

The Cookson family, photographed around 1900 at Pilling Hall Farm, which occupies the site of the grange from which the monks of Cockersand Abbey ran their Pilling estate.

CHAPTER 10

The Incumbents of Pilling

BEFORE the Dissolution of the Monasteries in 1539-1540, the Chapel at Pilling had been served by the canons of Cockersand, and from then by a Curate from the Rectory or Parish of Garstang, but in the year 1621 King James I ordered : " That from henceforth there shall bee a minister from time to time continually kept att the chappell of Pillyn," and although in 1650 we are told, " the inhabitants being very many humbly desire they may be made a Parish," there is every reason to believe there was a Curate officiating here in the year 1630, when the Registers of Christenings begin (Burials 1685).

John Lumley was Curate here in 1650, when he was " silenc'd for severall misdemeanors." Probably he was a follower of the Stuart cause. He was the Curate here during the terrible plague of that time. His signature is to be seen on Petitions to the Justices of Peace, dated the 6th and 10th July, 1650.

Little imagination is needed to visualise him visiting his stricken flock in their hovels, taking them food and comforting them in their pain and grief. A man of great courage, prepared to face death by a horrible disease or to be " silenc'd " for his principles.

Natha Halliwell. In the Registers of Christenings appears the entry " 1647 Natha Halliwell minister of Pilling 7th February." This is apparently a later insertion, as the ink is the same colour as an entry " Mem : June ye 19th, 1670. Natha Halliwell entered first at Pilling." He was married to Anne Cragg in Pilling Chapel on 10th December, 1670.

Oswald Croskell. In the Registers of Christenings appears : " Oswald Croskell minister of Pilling was baptised ye second of May in ye year of o^{r}Lord 1651." This was probably a later insertion.

Another entry is " Oswald Croskell curat de Pilling and Susannah Tomlinson was marryed ye 17th day of January anno 1675."

Richard Hardy. The Registers say " 1686 Nov. 28. James Bibby and Margaret Bibby marryed at Pilling Chapel by me Rd Hardy, Curate."

He was a graduate of Cambridge University. He became Rector of North Meols in 1688 and died there in 1708.

Gabriel Dawson was Curate from 28th January, 1687, until he died. He was buried at Pilling on 15th November, 1692.

Thomas Hunter probably followed immediately.

There are three references in the Registers :—
1. 1694, between 24th June and 18th Dec. " 24 per me in hoc folio sepulti fuerunt. Tho. Hunter." (24 were buried by me on this page).
2. 18th Jan., 1701. " Tho. Hunter Minister of Pilling & Margarett Yorke of Lancaster yᵉ eleaventh of January 1701 " were married.
3. Under Burials. 1715 Mrs. Margrett Hunter   1 Aprill
    Mr. Thomas Hunter   1 May

John Anyon was appointed to the Curacy on the 24th May, 1715, by Roger Hesketh and Edmund·Hornby. He did not " let the grass grow under his feet " for the next year he was heading a Petition to the Bishop of Chester for permission to build the " Old " Church and guaranteeing a sum of £300 for that purpose. His work of building the Old Church stands out all the more prominently if one remembers that in the early 18th century religion was at an extremely low ebb. Most of the religious Societies had almost ceased to function. And, as for the clergy, the majority would accumulate offices which they could not possibly perform, simply to augment their stipends, and quite honestly did not consider they were doing anything wrong. Indeed, the evils of pluralities and non-residence were most conspicuous among the bishops. In the year 1723 his son, Thomas Carter, was buried on 22nd February ; his daughter, Ann, on the 10th March ; his wife, Alice, on the 8th July, and his daughter, Jane, on the 7th October. He was Curate of Pilling until 1731 when he went to Ribby with Wrea. He died in 1770 at the ripe old age of 86 years.

John Coulton was Curate from September, 1731, until 1758. He was buried at Pilling on 20th February, 1758.

As Curates' stipends were so small, unless they had private means, it was necessary to supplement them by some means or other. Sometimes the Curate did a little farming. This seems to have been the case with the Rev. John Coulton. His estate consisted of " A House three Bays (rooms) Barn four Bays site garden and Holmes parrocks the Nickoe field in two parts the House field in two parts the little Kiln Field the great Kiln field in two parts the Marsh in two parts and the Bows Field containing twenty acres thirty six perches and a third part in Anne Heys fields, containing four acres."

He bequeathed two shillings and sixpence each to his sons, John and Thomas, and fifteen pounds apiece to William and Paul, who was a tallow chandler, and the residue to his loving son Harry.

Harry died and by will dated 16th September, 1764, bequeathed to his mother Margaret (who seemed to find some difficulty in signing her name) and his brother Paul all his lands in Pilling. Mrs. Coulton was in financial straits, so they sold the estate to Richard Tomlinson on 13th February, 1767, for £300.

George Holden was born in 1720 in Yorkshire. He held an

estate in the Parish of Slaidburn and was a master at the Free Grammar School of Bentham. He was appointed to the Curacy of Pilling on 11th May, 1758, and remained until September 1767, when he went to Tatham Fell. He died in May 1793, and was buried at Bentham.

He was a great mathematician and compiled " Holden's Tide Tables," which are used to this day. The people of Pilling like to think of him sitting on the Bridge watching and studying the tides, hoping that what he learned at Pilling contributed in a large measure to his success.

When he died he left to his son, the Rev. George Holden, " all my books, papers and instruments used in calculating the Liverpool Tide Table."

His son the Rev. Dr. George Holden, L.L.D., continued his work on Tide Tables.

In March, 1950, during cleaning operations in the Harbour Master's office at Fleetwood, a copy of the original Tide Table " Calculated by G. Holden, Clerk, according to the theory of R. Holden, teacher of Mathematics in Castle Street, Liverpool, was found." The table has been framed and hangs in the Harbour Master's Office at Fleetwood, a reminder of the great work carried out by a one-time Vicar of Pilling. The sun dial over the door of the Old Church was placed there to his memory.

Cuthbert Harrison was born in 1744 and was appointed to the Curacy on the 15th September, 1767. He took the Degree of B.A. at Trinity College in 1766. He died at Clifton in the parish of Kirkham on the 1st June, 1790, and was buried at Singleton, his native village.

John Hunter was appointed a Master at Kirkland School in 1737 and then Curate of St. Thomas' Church, Garstang, from which he resigned and went to Broughton in 1760. He was appointed to Pilling on 1st October, 1774, and died here, and was buried on 27th August, 1781. His wife, Jane, was buried here on 3rd June, 1775.

William Bateson was appointed on the 15th October, 1781, and was suspended on the 2nd March, 1792, " for drunkenness, neglect of his ministerial duties and also for enormous crimes "— so we pass on quickly.

Thomas Godfrey was appointed assistant Curate in 1795 and perpetual Curate on the 17th October, 1798, and resigned in 1802 to take up another living. He married Ann, the daughter of Richard Whiteside, who left her in his Will £50, also £100 to be paid by his Executors at the most useful and advantageous time during her natural life.

James Potter was appointed on the 8th December, 1802. He was the son of James Potter of Ellergill in the parish of Orton in Westmorland. He had been Curate at Woodplumpton. He died on the 30th September, 1825, aged 69 years. His grave is in the South-East corner of the churchyard. Many stories, which need not be repeated here, are told about him. Most of them are disparaging. He is said to have been a fighter and liked to see a cock fight (as did many other people at that time) and was even known to have offered to put " Half a crown on the red 'un." But it might be well to remember that at this time there was a tremendous religious revival in the birth of Wesleyan Methodism, whose followers frowned severely on such activities.

Allen Clarke, in his book *Windmill Land*, tells us that one of his parishioners said : " He were th' best preicher an' feighter as ever come t' Pilling." Clarke goes on to say : " A man may have many a worse epitaph than that."

Be it as it may, the church was so crowded that it was necessary to raise the roof and put in the gallery and moreover the work was completed within twelve months of receiving the Faculty, and—paid for !

In the Marriage Register appears the entry, " Rev. Jas Potter, Incumbent Minister of Pilling, Parish of Garstang and Chapelry of Pilling, widower and Margeret Tomlinson, spinster of this Chapelry were married in this Chapel by Licence with consent of Parents this Second day of June in the year one thousand eight hundred and fourteen by Rev. Jno. Miller of Stalmine."

In his Will he left all his estate to his wife Margaret, including his leasehold tenement at Lazy Hill, then in the tenure of Cuthbert Gardner, and if she had anything left, she to provide for his four children by a former marriage, in conjunction with her son, Richard Tomlinson, he having " so just an opinion of her integrity to make a fair disposal."

His first wife, Ann, was buried on the 28th April, 1814, aged 56, and his second, Margaret, on the 30th May, 1828.

James Dawson Banister. Until the 5th September, 1830, the Rev. J. D. Banister spelled his name with two " n "s and then onwards with one, probably reverting to the ancient form.

Born on 2nd March, 1798, in Yorkshire, of a family of very ancient lineage. He was educated at Sedberg Grammar School and studied at St. Bees' College. He was ordained Deacon in 1821 and priest the following year and then went to St. James' Church, Burton, in Kendal. He was appointed Ferpetual Curate of Pilling on the 27th November, 1825. On his arrival in Pilling, he found the so-called vicarage was merely a cottage in a ruinous condition. It is supposed to have been the present " Sandfield Cottage," but there is no evidence, yet, to confirm this. He soon had a substantial vicarage built (1831) in a central position and put the glebe and its buildings in order.

He was a great educationist and set to work to build schools both in Pilling and Eagland Hill. To quote his own words : " They had only indifferent schools—small, dirty and quite unfit for the purpose." The National School was erected in 1856. He was presented in September, 1861, with a beautiful solid silver card tray, made by J. Mater of Liverpool, and a purse by " The Inhabitants, Owners of Property and Others interested in Pilling, as a token of their regard and high appreciation of his services in procuring the erection of the new school."

In 1870, with the active assistance of his son, Rev. E. D. Banister, who was acting as his Curate, he was responsible for the erection of the Mission Church at Eagland Hill, which was opened on the 28th April, 1870. A salver was presented to him in April, 1870, probably to mark the occasion.

In 1871 the Eagland Hill School was erected.

The " Old " church yard was extended in 1862.

On Advent Sunday, 1875, he had completed fifty years of ministerial labours as Vicar. On Monday afternoon, the 13th December, he was presented with a handsome Testimonial and a purse of five hundred guineas as a token of respect for his Christian character and high appreciation of the good work he had accomplished during his long period of labour.

The Address is as follows :—

To the Rev. James Dawson Banister, Vicar of Pilling, in the County of Lancaster.

Reverend and Dear Sir,

We your parishioners and friend, offer you our most hearty congratulations on the completion of fifty years' service in this Parish. We desire to express our high sense of your faithfulness to your duties, and your unwearied kindness to the sick, aged and poor. You have been unceasing in your efforts to promote the welfare of all. By your instrumentality the present National Schools were erected in 1856, and under your constant supervision have been amongst the most efficient in the County. One portion of your Parish has from a wild moss and bog become a fruitful field and you have taken active interest in all which has converted this large uncultivated unhabited tract of land into rich fields and homesteads. It now through your care possesses an excellent Mission Chapel and Schools. We trust you may live many years amongst us assured of the continual affection and esteem of all, and we beg your acceptance of the accompanying Purse of 500 guineas as an earnest of the same.

Signed on behalf of the subscribers the 13th day of December, 1875.

R. C. Gardner, Chairman.

John S. Gardner	Harri Edwards	Thos. Corless
C. S. Bagot	Wm. Shepherd	Joseph Gornall
Andrew Kay	R. Preston	W. Jenkinson
	Henry T. Barton, Treasurer.	
	Thos. Nicholson, Secretary.	

The following lines were written on the Commemoration of the Rev. J. D. Banister's fiftieth year as Vicar of Pilling, by

John Isles, Farmer :—
    I sing not of honours attained in the field,
    Where rapine and strife their red banners display.
    The beauties and graces which virtue doth yield
    Are the sources, the theme, and the force of my lay.

    Our army may boast of its shot and its shell.
    Our commerce may trust in the wealth of its mines.
    But the high hopes of Britain, our sages will tell,
    Exist in the work of her earnest divines.

    Yea mount Fancy's stage in a retrograde form
    And view the gross darkness of mediaeval times.
    See ignorance sweep through the land like a storm
    Desecrating Religion with horrible crimes.

    Now Truth, glorious star ! So refulgently shines,
    And learning, and art are so fast gaining ground,
    That Ignorance baffled gives palpable signs
    Ere long its base presence will scarcely be found.

    And thou native village, where honesty dwells,
    Fifty years thy auricular powers have been charged,
    With teaching, which all teaching excels,
    No wonder thy morals are greatly enlarged.

    Yea Pilling, the pith of thy warmest esteem,
    Thy eloquent Vicar may worthily claim,
    All rules for thy weal emanated from him,
    If woes thou hast still 'tis thyself to blame.

    For ages to come let thy piety shine,
    As proof of his worth, his zeal to commend,
    His actions portray that in him combine
    The diligent pastor, the generous friend.

He acted as agent to the Lords of the Manor and through his influence large tracts of land were reclaimed, whilst under his supervision, and often from his plans, healthy and convenient farm houses and cottages replaced the old peat-walled, heather-thatched hovels, daubed and floored with clay. His influence with the owners, also was the means of hedgerows being substituted for banks of earth.

He was a keen observer of natural history and an enthusiastic antiquarian. He had close contacts with eminent scholars on these subjects and contributed written articles to learned societies on matters of local interest.

It is interesting to note he introduced the chanting of the

Psalms and, to quote his own words, " though some of the old people might have objected to the change," he felt " that now nine out of every ten members of the congregation would say that it was a beneficial one. It has conduced to the popularity of the services, without introducing novelties into the Church service or anything contrary to the Prayer Book."

He retired in 1876, at the age of 78 years, on account of advancing age and failing strength and went to reside with his son, the Rev. E. D. Banister, at Whitechapel, after fifty-one years' service.

He passed suddenly to his rest on the 9th January, 1883, in his 85th year, and is buried in Pilling church yard.

John Wilson Waithman was appointed Vicar in 1876. He came from Yealand. His great work was the building of the new church. His efforts to bring this to fruition were enormous. He acted as Chairman and Secretary of the Building Committee until his health broke. The splendid edifice, the Church, can, with truth, be said to be the Rev. John Wilson Waithman's memorial. He died on the 27th January, 1893, aged 46 years, and was buried at Yealand Conyers in the church-yard of the Society of Friends. Many Pilling people attended his funeral.

At a Vestry Meeting held on Friday, 7th April, 1893, Mr. Corless moved and Mr. W. Curwen seconded the following Resolution : " That this Meeting desires to express its regret at the death of the late Vicar, the Rev. J. W. Waithman, and its appreciation of his services rendered during the seventeen years he was Vicar of the Parish."

Richard Titley Gardner. " Parson Dick," as he was known, was Vicar of Pilling from 1893 to 1897. He was the son of the Rev. James Cardwell Gardner and grandson of Mr. R. C. Gardner. He was born at Fluke Hall and baptised in the " Old " church. He was a great " sport," keen on boxing and football and played with the youths on Saturday afternoons. Both he and his father went to considerable trouble collecting and listing documents which belonged to the Church or Overseers. Those of the latter were handed over to the Parish Council when it was first formed in 1894.

He was a chaplain in the Boer War and was mentioned in despatches by Lord Kitchener. He was Secretary of the Central Board of Missions of the Church of England and visited all the Colonial Dioceses prior to the Pan-Anglican Congress in 1908. He spent some time in Australia and during the 1914-1918 war was a Chaplain in the army.

He went to Chertsey, Surrey, where he died on the 1st October, 1934, and was buried in St. Steven's Burial Ground on the 5th October.

Thomas Pearson was appointed Vicar of Pilling on 4th July, 1897. He took his degree of B.A. at Christ's College, Cambridge, in 1888 and his M.A. in 1892.   He was made a deacon in 1888 and ordained Priest in 1890.   He was formerly at the Church of St. Matthew, Chadderton, 1888-93.

He really made Pilling known through his creation of Pilling Vicarage rose gardens.   During his incumbency the vicarage was extended at a cost of £1,200 ; the organ was installed ; also the reredos in memory of those who made the supreme sacrifice in the 1914-1918 war.

He died on the 20th August, 1924, and was buried on the 23rd August.

Percy Gresty followed Rev. T. Pearson. He took his L.Th. in 1916 and was made a deacon in 1916, and ordained Priest in 1917.

He was at Colne from 1916 to 1920 and Burnley from 1920 to 1922.   He was appointed Curate of St. Oswald's, Preesall (the first) in 1922 and remained until 1924.   He was instituted Vicar of Pilling on the 25th November, 1924 and remained until 19th January, 1930. He was Vicar of Gannow from 1930 to 1937 and Great Harwood from 1937 until 1945, but was Chaplain in the army from 1941 until 1945.   He was appointed Vicar of Inskip in 1946.

Myles Atkinson was educated at St. John's College, Cambridge. He took his B.A. degree in 1906 and his M.A. in 1910.   He was made a deacon in 1908 and Priest in 1909.   He was curate of St. Ambrose's Church, Pendleton, from 1908 to 1911, and was appointed curate of Christ's Church, Salford, in 1911.

He became Vicar of Woodborough in Nottingham, and was instituted Vicar of Pilling on 3rd March, 1930, and was incumbent until February, 1949, when he resigned for health reasons.   He died at Salford on 21st February and was buried at Dalton-in-Furness on Monday, 25th February, 1952.

Roy Ashworth Kennedy was instituted to the living of Pilling on the 27th August, 1949. He entered Lincoln Theological College in 1943, was made deacon in 1945 and ordained Priest in 1946.

He was Curate of Kirkham from 1945 until 1947 and Fleetwood from 1947 until his appointment to Pilling. He resigned on Easter Day, 13th April, 1952, to take up work in Trinidad.

Idris Owen Evans studied at St. Michael's College, Llandaff, and was made deacon in 1927 and ordained Priest in 1928.   He was Curate of Llaniled with Llanharan from 1927 to 1928 and granted permission to officiate at Buckingham during 1928 and 1929.   He was Curate of Pontefract from 1929 to 1930 and Tarvin (in charge of Kelsall) from 1930 to 1931, and Goole from 1931 to 1933.   He was appointed Vicar of Newton-on-Ouse in 1933 and remained there until his appointment to Ironville in 1936, and went to South Darley as Vicar in 1947.

He was instituted to the Vicarage of Pilling by the Lord Bishop of Blackburn and inducted by the Rural Dean of Garstang, the Rev. John Moss, Vicar of Bilsborrow, on the 19th July, 1952.

Chapter 11

Chapel Wardens of the Chapelry of Pilling

There is no record available before 1721.

1721 Richard Tomlinson, Chris. Clarke. (His son's name is on the grave stone in the old Chapel yard at Newers Wood.)
1722 Robert Hey, John ——.
1723 William Bollin, Arthur Smith.
1724 Robert Smithson, Geo. Pedder.
1726 Robert Hey, Henry Bibby.
1727   do.   do.
1728 Rd. Benner, Jno. Burton.
1729 Thos. Eskham, Thos. Wilkinson.
1730 Francis Bond, ——.
1731 Henry Bibby, Robert Sanderson.
1732
1733 William Bagot, William Noar.
1734 John Herdman, William Smith.
1735 Peter Threlfall Danson, ——
1736 Wm. Smith, Chr. Bond.
1737 William Hoole, Crofter Smith.
1738 William Hoole, Crofter Smith.
1739 Tho. Taylor, James Hey.
1741 Henry Smith, John Smith.
1742 James Bibby, Jno. Hodgkinson.
1743 Richard Tomlinson, Xtopher Gardner.
1744 Robert Smithson, Tho. Johnes.
1745 Robert Whiteside, William Cokell.
1746 John Hey, James Holme.
1747 Richard Clark, John Hey.
1748 John Blackon, Peter Basford.
1749 Thomas. Bond, Edmd. Taylor.
1750 John Corless, George Moore.
1751 John Taylor, John Heys.
1752 John France, Robert Smithson.
1753 Robert Smithson, John France.
1754 Willm. Corless, Robert Smithson.
     Note—5/- was paid "To Mr. Coulton at Pilling Feast." This is the first known mention of Pilling Feast. Also "To fensing the Chappel yard in, and lying a plat in the Chappel lane 1/-."
1755 Robert Whiteside. John Heys.
1756 John Hey, Richard Bagat.

1757 William Corless, Ambrose Parker.
1758 James Tomlinson, William Preston.
1759 Geo. Addison, Jno. Tomlinson.
1760 Robert Whiteside, Jno. France.
1761
1762 Richard Tomlinson, James Heys.
1763 Robert Heys, Wm. Noar.
1764 John Bradshaw, Henry Herdman.
1765 Henry Threlfall, Robert Heys.
1766 James Smith, Ralph Croft.
1767 James Hey, Thomas Wilkinson.
1768 Tho. Eskham, Thos. Dickinson.
1769 Richard Tomlinson, Thomas Taylor.
1770 Richard Tomlinson (Sen.), Thoms. Eskham.
1771 Richard Bago', John Gardner.
1772 Richard Whiteside, Will Mason.
1773 William Marshel, Thomas Gill.
1774 Richard Tomlinson, Junr., Thomas Smith.
1775 Christopher Gardner, Richard Whiteside.
1776 John Naylor, John Carter.
1777 Richard Tomlinson, Sen., for his own Estate and James Tomlinson, Junr., for Holmes' Estate.
1778 William Wilkinson and Robert Dickson for own Estate.
1779 Thomas Corless for Magdalene Bell's and Geo. Moore for Bone-hill.
1780 Gawin Herdman for Lucas's, and Robert Heys, Senr., for his own Estate.
1781 Richard Tomlinson, Senr., for Blackburn's, and Robert Preston for his own Esta e.
1782 John France for his own Estate, and Robt. Heys, Senr., for his own.
1783 John Eskham and John Whiteside each for his own Estate. The Church Rate increased this year from 1d. to 1½d. per acre.
1784 Peter Fisher for John Leech and Wm. Smith for his own.
1785 Richard Bagot and Wm. Bradshaw each for his own Estate.
1786 James Tomlinson for Dickinson's Estate and Peter Fisher for Blacows.
1787 Gawin Herdman for his own Estate and Wm. Croft for Bennet's.
1788 Robert Dickson for Carr House and Geo. Dickinson for his own house.
1789 John Bagot for Saunderson's and Thos. Corless for Ridge.
1790 Wm. Shaw for his own and John Mount for John Bond's.
1791 Thompson Noar for his own Estate and Robert Tomlinson for Eskham House.
1792 Robert Tomlinson for Blackburn's and James Smith for his own Estate.

1793   Robt. Whiteside for Richard Whiteside's Estate and John Dickinson for his own.

1794   Thomas Corless for Ridge and Henry Threlfall for his own Estate.

1795   Robert Dickson for his own Estate and Robt. Heys for his own Estate.

1796   John Heys for his own Estate and Thos. Higginson for Richard Tomlinson.

1797   Richd. Whiteside and Gawin Herdman, each for his own Estate.

1798   Willm. Mason for his own Estate and Cuthbert Gardner for Jane Bradshaw's.

1799   Willm. Bond for his own Estate and George Lancaster for Cumpsteys.

1800   Robt. Bibby for Thos. Miller's Estate and Robt. Mount for Mrs. Bibby's Estate.

1801   William Wilkinson for his own Estate and Willm. Bamber for Singleton's.

1802-1803   Thomas for his own Estate and Mattw. Bradshaw for Thos. Bradshaw's.   On 8th April 4/6 was paid to Ann Potter for washing surplices 4 times and mending.

1804-1805   John Whiteside, Junr., for his father's Estate and Lawrence Dickson for Robert Porter Senr.

1806   Richard Whiteside for Smallwood Hey and George Moor for Bone Hill.

1807   Thomas Corless for (Miss) Magdelene Bell's and John Wilkinson for James Curwen's.
       It is from Miss Magdelene Bell's (sister of William Bell Corless) name that " Maudlands " farm takes its name.

1808   ——

1809   ——

1810   Willm. Bradshaw and John Bibby for their own Estate.

1811   Willm. Dickson for Richard Readman's Estate and Willm. Bimson for John Bourn's (?).

1812   John Tomlinson for Smallwood Hey and John Corles for his own Estate.

1813   John Tomlinson and Thomas Bagot.

1814   Robert Whiteside and Thomas Bagot.
       8/- was paid for straw for the school (thatching).   The school was burned down this year.

1815   Robert Whiteside and Thos. Bagot.

1816   Lawrence Dickson and Wm. Mackneal.

1817   Thos. Preston and Wm. Mackneal.

1818   ,,   ,,   ,,   ,,

1819   ,,   ,,   ,,   ,,

1820   ,,   ,,   ,,   ,,

1821   John Dickinson and Richard Higginson.

1822   Richard Higginson and Thomas Carter.

From now detailed items of the Chapel Wardens accounts are available and make very interesting reading. A very startling item is £6 . 9 . 0 for wine to Thomas Carter. The price of wine in 1826 was 14/- and 16/- per gallon. This would, therefore, represent a consumption of eight or nine gallons per annum. The cost of wine the next year was £8 . 18 . 9. There must have been a very large number of Communicants ! This is borne out by the cost of bread, which was 7/- paid to Arthur Simpson. Yet it appears the Incumbents were paid for five Sacraments a year only, at 2/6 per Sacrament. We do know that during " Parson " Potter's incumbency it was necessary to raise the roof of the chapel and erect a gallery.

The cost of rushes for the chapel floor was 10/-.

The amount paid by the Wardens for the destruction of sparrows, of course varied. This year it was £2 . 8 . 2. A half-penny was paid for one sparrow.

1823   Peter Parr and John Sykes.
£1 rent was paid to the Minister, for the old chapel yard (in Newers Wood). This was in accordance with the Petition of 3rd October, 1716, to the Bishop of Chester.

1824   Peter Parr served for John Williamson's Estate and Thos. Wilkinson for his own.
The Ringers were paid 2/- and Singers 2/6.

1825   Peter Parr for Christopher Bond's Estate and William Corless for his own.

1826   Peter Kellrick for his own Estate and Thos. Gardner for Pilling Hall Estate.
£4 . 12 . 0 was paid for an iron chest. This is probably the small safe in the vestry of the new church.
4/8 was paid for 4 " windles " of lime. A windel (Anglo-Saxon) was a woven basket and would hold about 220 lbs. of wheat.
James Curwen, a skilled mason, was paid 5/- for 2 days' work.

1827   John Cookson for Gawin Herdman's Estate and John Dickson for Carr House Estate.
£4 . 18 . 11 was paid for sparrows this year.

1828   James Atkinson for Bennet's and Christopher Parkinson for Bibby's Estate.

1829   John Tomlinson for his own Estate and James Bradshaw for Will Bradshaw's Estate.
£5 . 14 . 9 paid for sparrows this year—at ½d. each, that is 2,754 sparrows !

1830   John Tomlinson for William Corless' Estate and John Ronson for Dickinson's Estat.e
4/6 was paid for cleaning the sun dial.

1831   John Tomlinson and John Ronson.
This year 2 new bells were bought for £12. Taking down the bells cost 2/2.

1833   John Tomlinson and John Ronson.
1834   ,,   ,,   ,,   ,,
1835   Thos. Wilkinson and Robert Butler.
1836   James Clifton and Thos. Corless.
        2/- was paid for coal.
1837   James Clifton and Thos. Carter.
        This year coal cost 3/6.
1838   Robert Alty and Willm. Bimson.
        Candles were rather expensive—7d. per lb. 5 lbs. were
        bought this year, but only 2 lbs. in 1839.
1839   William Bell Corless and Richard Dunderdale.
1840   ,,   ,,   ,,   ,,   ,,
1841   William Clarkson and James Butler.
        Paid £1 . 15 . 0 to the mole catcher.
1842   John Parkinson and Robert Bradley.
        Wm. Preston was paid 2/- for " getting rush out of the
        Chapel " and 1/- was paid for ridding snow in the Chapel
        Lane.
1843   Christopher Myers and Robt. Rawcliffe.
        Labour was evidently very cheap.   6d. was paid for " Fencing
        Chapel Yard " ; 9d. " To carting rough cast to Chapel " ;
        7d. " To repairing Chapel door."
1844   Thomas Bourne and Thomas Baogot.
        John Bradshaw was paid " 4s. for 2 days' work at 2/-."
1845-1847   Richard Alty and John Bradshaw.
1848   Christopher Myers and George Carter.
1849-1850   Christopher Myers and William Bimson.
        On the 3rd May, 1850, £3 . 6 . 9d was paid to Jas. Butler
        (he did the wood work for the National School) for
        new doors.
1851   Christopher Myers and Wm. Bimson.
1852   William Bimson and Jerimiah Parkinson.
        The Sexton's salary seems to have been £2 . 1 . 0 per annum,
        as this amount was paid to " John Bradshaw, Sexton's
        Salary."
1853   William Bimson and Jerimiah Parkinson.
1854   ,,   ,,   ,,   ,,
1855   ,,   ,,   ,,   ,,
        The bill for coal, coke and carriage was £1 . 8 . 10½.
        (In the year 1950 it was £60 . 0 . 10 !)
        10s. seems to have been paid annually to the Wardens for
        their salary.
1856   William Bimson and Jerimiah Parkinson.
1857-1859   Richard Kay and Robert Clifton.
1860-1882   William Shepherd and Robert Preston.
1883   William Shepherd.
1884-1888   William Shepherd and Richard Kay.
1889

1890
1891
1892
1893
1894   This year £21.5.0 was paid to Wm. Throughton for 425 shrubs.
1895
1896   Thomas Corless and Joseph Holden.
1897   „   „   „   „
1898   „   „   „   „
1899   Thomas Corless and Thomas Shepherd.
1900   James Bradley and Thomas Shepherd.
1901-02 „   „   „   „
1903   „   „   „   „
1904   T. A. Fairclough and Richard Parkinson.
1905   „   „   „
1906-1909 John Rossall and Richard Parkinson.
1910   Thomas Richards and John Kellet.
1911   „   „   „   „
1912   Thomas Richards.
1913   Thomas Richards and John Kellet.
1914-1915 John Rossall and John Kellet.
1916   James Carter and Thomas Lawrenson.
1917   „   „   „   „
1918   James Carter and Henry Curwen.
1919-1926 Henry Curwen and Thomas Richards.
1926-1927 Richard Kellet and Thomas Richards.
1927-1941 Richard Kellet and Thomas Lawrenson.
1941-1947 Richard Kellet and James Carter.
1947-1949 Richard Kellet and Frederick J. Sobee.
1949   Joseph Hall and F. J. Sobee.

In 1751 the Calendar was reformed. Until then the year began officially on March 25th, so that the day after March 24th, 1750, was March 25th, 1751—although Jan. 1st was called New Year's Day. That is why up to this time events taking place in January, February, or March sometimes have the official date of the old year, and sometimes the popular date of the new year, e.g. Robert Carter, by Will, dated 31st January, 1710 (Old Style) or 1711 (New Style). This must always be borne in mind and applies to the dates given above so that up to the year 1751 one year should be added as the dates given are those when the Church Wardens ceased to be in office, which was on the 24th March. That is the reason why the Annual Vestry Meeting is still held about this time. After 1751 "O.S." disappeared altogether, so that the above dates right themselves about 1762.

D

CHAPTER 12

Wesleyan Methodism

AT no time since the heathen Danes, probably, was there, in English history such a period as the eighteenth century when social conditions and religious zeal had sunk so low. Whichever way we turn we find the same horrible story of brutality, lethargy and self-satisfaction.

The debtors' prisons were hot beds of vice. The prisons produced criminals instead of deterring them. The criminal laws were out of all reason, hanging and transporting human beings for the least excuse. Slavery was rampant, even religious societies owned slaves. Little effort was made to provide the rapidly increasing population of the towns with schools and churches (thanks to the Rev. John Anyon, this does not apply to Pilling), yet the Georgian mansions were being built in many parts of the country.

In most parishes the Sacrament was only celebrated three times in the year—in Pilling it was celebrated five times.

When George I ascended the throne in 1714, he threw in his lot with the Whigs. They were opposed to anything which savoured of Jacobitism and therefore Roman Catholicism, and leaned to the Protestant Non-conformists and Parliament passed legislation granting religious toleration.

This provided an opportunity for a champion of the Christian religion to come forth into the lists—John Wesley.

John Wesley attended a meeting of the Moravians in London. He experienced a spiritual " new birth " and felt " my heart strangely warmed. I felt I did trust in Christ, Christ alone, for salvation, and that an assurance was given to me that He had taken away my sins and saved me from the law of sin and death." In 1739 he began to preach in the open air at Bristol, but was not satisfied. He wanted to spread his message throughout England.

The effect of his preaching was phenomenal. Thousands were converted. To do this he travelled five thousand miles a year and it is said he preached more than 40,000 sermons. On one of his journeys North he stayed at Brook House, Brock, and sowed seeds there which before long germinated and bore fruit in Pilling. At first he formed small societies but the number of converts grew to such an extent that it was necessary to have some form of organisation, and the Methodist Society grew up. The original name was " The people called Methodists." There was no thought in Wesley's mind of breaking from the mother Church, in fact, only a short time before his death, he begged his followers, " Be Church

The Old Wesleyan Methodist Chapel.

The Wesleyan Methodist Chapel and Sunday School.

of England men still." He died in 1791 and after his death the
" Wesleyan Methodist Church " was founded. This was the
official title of this particular form of Methodism. The Church of
England had no answer, separation was inevitable.

In 1758 there were two Protestant Dissenting families in
Pilling. The pioneer of Wesleyan Methodism in Pilling was Richard
Mason. He was a shoemaker, and was born in 1780. He was a
great reader, a great thinker and a diligent seeker after the truth.
In his search for the truth he would walk great distances to hear
a sermon. He once walked to Liverpool to hear Dr. Adam Clarke
preach.

One Sunday morning in the Autumn of 1811, he rose about
four o'clock and walked to Preston to hear a Methodist sermon
in the morning, and attended a Methodist " love feast " in the
afternoon, and as a result of his experiences there, his soul received
the spiritual re-birth, which Wesley taught was so necessary. He
came home overjoyed that at last he had been regenerated and
could now begin a new spiritual life. His wife shared his joy and
became his partner in his pioneer work. They passed on their
zeal to their friends and neighbours and soon an enthusiastic little
society was formed.

The first meeting was held in Richard Mason's house in
December, 1811. The members were, Richard Mason, Hannah
Mason, Peter Parr, George and Agnes McNeal, James McNeal,
William McNeal, Jenny Cornall, William Bell Threlfall and Robert
Hey. These were the founders of the church which to-day stands
strong and firm in Pilling.

Richard Mason died in 1858 and his wife in 1855.

Before very long, in 1812, a site was obtained for the erection
of a Chapel. This was on the westward side of Wheel Lane, near
Chapel House. The land was conveyed by Christopher Parkinson
and his wife, Alice (formerly Alice Crookhall, widow) of Whitting-
ham to the following Trustees : William Smith, William Bell
Threlfall, Robert Hey, William McNeal, Peter Parr, James McNeal
(all of Pilling), Thomas Gaskell of Brickhouse, Hambleton, Thomas
Preston, of Stalmine, James Roskell of Thorton, Richard Nagg
of Garstang, mole catcher, John Leece and John Howard of Preston.

The Deed is dated 30th June, 1812. £6 was paid for the land,
which was 486 square yards.

The work of building the chapel was begun towards the end
of 1812. It was called the Meadow and was formerly the Estate
and Inheritance of John Sumner, father of Alice Parkinson. The
contract was given to John Lambert, who had the contract for
raising the roof of the " Old " church and putting in the gallery.
The stone work was done by James Curwen.

The contract was for £334 but there were extra expenses
amounting to £22 . 1 . 2½. The work was completed in 1813.
£200, raised mainly by subscription, was paid off, the balance

being paid off later.

The chapel was opened on the 12th September, 1813. The collection amounted to £8 . 16 . 5½.

The chapel was a plain building, constructed of stone from Richmond delph in Forton. It was white-washed outside and plastered inside. It seated 250. When it was first built it had a single aisle running down the centre, but later this was filled with high-backed pews and two side aisles were made. There was a gallery across the south end. The pulpit was at the north end. The windows were provided with shutters to protect them from being broken by those who did not favour the early Methodists. The floor was at first covered with rushes, but in 1832 the Rev. Isaac Dennison, who was then the Minister, had a wooden floor put down. At the same time the vestry was moved from the south-west corner of the chapel and a new one built at the north end. Until the first Sunday in January, 1869, when a new harmonium was installed, the choir was accompanied by a bass fiddle and sometimes a flute and a clarinet.

By 1886 the congregations had grown to such an extent that a meeting of officials, members, seat holders and others interested, was held to consider the question of building another chapel on a new site, but the majority of the people present were in favour of enlarging the present building. Another meeting was held, but although £250 was promised the matter was allowed to lie in abeyance for another six years.

The first Sunday School was established on the 25th March, 1821. Instruction in writing was given, as it was at the National Sunday School. Richard Mason and James McNeal were the first Superintendents. William McNeal, William B. Threlfall, and Sarah Hayes were among the Teachers.

During the next ten years two hundred and seventeen scholars were enrolled. In 1831 there were fifty-seven scholars and eight teachers. James Threlfall was appointed Superintendent towards the end of 1831.

In 1833 the Committee consisted of James Threlfall, George McNeal, Thomas Walmesly, James Houghton and Elizabeth Threlfall.

Andrew Kay was appointed Superintendent in 1846 and held the position until 1870. Up to this time the Superintendent carried out the work of Secretary and Treasurer, but on the 20th May, 1870, John Fisher was appointed Treasurer and William Bradshaw Secretary. They gave this work up in December, 1870, and were succeeded by Thomas Clarkson and Henry Curwen, who was also appointed Superintendent.

In 1881 there were eight teachers and fifty-eight scholars.

At the Annual School Party in 1887, the Junior Superintendent, in a speech, remarked upon the success of scholars who had passed through the school. " There were three local preachers on the platform. There were preachers in the Garstang Circuit ; two in the Blackpool, and one in the Lancaster, and one in the Liverpool Circuits. Then there was that most outstanding preacher, Rev. T. T. Lambert, and in foreign fields was the Rev. Henry Threlfall, and in Australia, still carrying on his work at the age of seventy-five was the Rev. James Houghton."

A very remarkable record, but the full story had not been told.

From 1836 the Wesleyan movement has been associated with the Temperance movement, but in the early days it did not receive much encouragement. The Trustees of the Chapel would not allow meetings to be held in the chapel until the Wesleyan Conferance decided that all chapels should be used for temperance work.

The Pilling enthusiasts, not to be deterred, following the example of their teacher, Wesley, held their meetings in the open air or in barns—in Smallwood Hey, in a house and barn belonging to John Bradshaw. (It stood where Mr. W. Rossall's house is now ; there is a stone built in this house from the old barn.) Meetings were also held at Scronkey, in a barn belonging to James Threlfall. The prime movers were William Sherdley, T. T. Lambert, Henry Curwen and Henry Threlfall. They had their first meeting in George McNeal's barn. On the occasion of the visit of the Rev. Dr. Gale, by the permission of the Rev. J. D. Banister, a Temperance meeting was held in the National school. The Rev. J. D. Banister gave his active and sympathetic support by acting as Chairman, and allowing Dr. Gates to preach two temperance sermons in the Parish Church.

T. T. Lambert left Pilling to take up the ministry ; Henry Threlfall went abroad ; William Sherdley went to Fleetwood as Town Missionary and died on the 2nd January, 1866.

On the 1st July the Rev. John Leathley convened a public meeting in the chapel, at which it was unanimously agreed to form a Temperance Society and Band of Hope in connection with the Wesleyan Church.

Rev. J. Leathley was elected President ; W. G. Parsonson and Henry Curwen vice-Presidents ; Richard Parkinson Treasurer, and W. R. Curwen Secretary.

In the first year fifty-seven were enrolled in the Temperance Society and sixty-seven in the Band of Hope.

Charles E. Curwen later became Secretary and continued until he died when he was succeeded by his brother, Martin Luther Curwen, who died on 27th Jan., 1928.

The question of building a new chapel was again raised. Mr. John Fisher bought the present site from Major Hornby and presented it to the Chapel Trustees.

Mr. J. Nuttall of Blackpool was appointed Architect.

On Wednesday, the 10th August, 1892, Memorial stones of the new chapel were laid. In the evening the Rev. T. T. Lambert gave an address in the old chapel.

Mr. Luther Curwen carried out a remarkable piece of work by doing the masonry. There is a story told that he wanted to lay every stone himself and thought he had done so, but a relative, who had been helping him, came back and laid a stone himself and so Luther Curwen laid every stone himself with the exception of one, which was rather a pity. Nevertheless, it is a splendid memorial to him.

The wood work was carried out by Thomas Shepherd and Sons of Pilling—another fine piece of work ; and the plastering by T. Cross and Sons of Lancaster.

The Rev. W. B. Butler, the Minister at that time, was not able to see the work completed, as his term of duty had come to an end. His place was taken by Rev. Wright Shovelton, and he was able to see the work brought to a successful conclusion.

On Wednesday, 13th June, 1894, Miss Lancaster, of Burnley, formally declared the Church open for public worship, and the first public service was held, Rev. T. T. Lambert being the preacher, as he also was when the Dedicatory Services were continued.

The Trustees were £1,000 in debt, so a Bazaar was held on the 9th, 10th and 11th June, 1896, and as a result of this and other gifts, the debt was reduced to £400. Another Bazaar was held in the National School on the 7th, 8th and 10th August, 1907, and the remaining debt was cleared off.

The next work which was undertaken was the building of the Sunday School. Mr. A. Simpson took down the old chapel, assisted by Mr. E. Curwen, and bought the stones, which were used in building the wall around the play-grounds of the National School in 1904. With a view to raising funds for this object, a Bazaar was held in the National School on 11th, 12th and 14th August, 1909.

It was opened on 11th by Mr. Joseph Cross, on the 12th by Mr. Nicholas Holden, and the 14th by Mr. Arnold Sarson, M.A., of Blackpool.

The foundation stone of this school was laid on 7th March, 1923, by the Rev. J. E. Wakerly, President of the Wesleyan Conference. The new Wesleyan Sunday School was opened on the 9th January, 1924, by Lady Kay, wife of Sir Richard Newbold Kay, M.P., and daughter of the Rev. T. T. Lambert.

The building is of Longridge stone and is roofed with Westmorland green slates. It will accommodate three hundred people. The estimated cost was £2,898, the furnishings bringing the total cost to £3,118 . 6 . 0, of which £2,400 had been paid.

The architects were Messrs. Potts and Hemmings of Manchester and Bolton, and the contractors were Messrs. J. Cartmell and Son of Preston.

So the trickle of Wesleyan Methodism became a flood. Helped by such tributaries as the Pilling Society, in two hundred years the stream of Wesleyan Methodists in Great Britain numbered almost half-a-million.

LOCAL METHODIST PREACHERS

Methodism in Pilling has produced a remarkable number of Local Preachers, men who have been prepared to sacrifice much to keep the flame of their religion burning brightly. Unfortunately, most of the records of Wesleyan Methodism seem to have been lost, so it is possible that some names have been unavoidably omitted which should have been included.

No doubt the early pioneers produced their quota, but the earliest names to be recorded are those of Threlfall (probably Lawrence, son of the early pioneer, William Bell Threlfall) and Houghton. These names appear in the Circuit Plan for Garstang for 1834.

Adam Houghton was a local preacher for nearly sixty years and during that time travelled thousands of miles to fulfil his engagements. He was born on the 8th March, 1816, and died on the 7th March, 1906, and so missed his ninetieth birthday by one day.

There is also the name of W. Percy on the Preston Plan of 1847. He was certainly a preacher some time before this, as he was then on full plan. He removed to Poulton-le-Fylde.

Thomas Tomlinson follows on full plan. He was the son of William and Alice Tomlinson and was born on the 18th April, 1820. He married Margaret, daughter of James McNeal, and later resided at Thornton, in the Blackpool Circuit, but often preached at Pilling. Mr. T. Parkinson Tomlinson of Poulton was his grandson and a worthy successor.

Robert Percy is a well known name to Pilling Methodists. Although Robert Percy lived for a considerable time at Lancaster he never lost his love for his native village, and when he retired from business he returned and resided in Fisher's Row. He continued his work as a Local Preacher until he died on Monday, 26th November, aged 77 years.

William McNeal, although of Pilling Lane, should be included. He was a son of the pioneer William McNeal. He was an excellent preacher and devoted to the work and held most of the offices open to a layman in the Methodist Church.

Henry Threlfall, a son of James Threlfall and grandson of William B. Threlfall, did loyal service for his church until he emigrated to America and became a minister.

Thomas Thornton Lambert was an outstanding man. He was the son of James and Alice Lambert and was born in a cottage on Lazy Hill on the 16th July, 1840. He was brought up by his sister Betty (Elizabeth, christened 20th January, 1833). He entered the ministry in 1867 and took charge of some of the foremost circuits during his ministerial career, and was at the Wesley Chapel, City Road, London—a very high honour indeed. His daughter married Sir Robert Newbold Kay. He was taken ill at the Conference held in London in 1906 and died shortly afterwards.

Seraiah Butler was a local preacher for many years. He was a very fluent and popular speaker. He died in a London hospital following an operation.

James Gardner and Benjamin Alty were also local preachers for some years.

James McNeal, a son of James McNeal of Pilling Lane, was another preacher. He emigrated to Australia and died suddenly shortly after his arrival there.

In the Garstang Circuit were two local preachers, both born in Pilling—Christopher McNeal, a grandson of James McNeal the elder, who resided at Forton, and Leonard Billington, who lived at Forton. George Henry McNeal, a cousin of Christopher became a minister at the City Road Chapel. He lectured in America and was considered a prospective candidate for the Presidency but he died.

In the Blackpool Circuit were two local preachers who were both born in Pilling—James Hayes and T. D. Mason, who was a great-grandson of Richard and Hannah Mason.

Another great-grandson of these pioneers was William Simpson, who was in the Lancaster Circuit.

Still another great-grandson of Richard and Hannah Mason is the Rev. Charles Sherdley, who, although he took a living at Bolton-le-Sands, still keeps a friendly eye directed across the Bay towards the place of his birth. His brother, William Sherdley, born at Sandside Farm, was also a local preacher. He went to reside at Preesall.

A name to be respected and kept in memory is that of John Preston, who was born on 31st October, 1868, and died on the 12th December, 1943. He was a man of great integrity, a man with whom it was a privilege to have been associated. He delighted in study and carried on his work to the end.

Another highly esteemed preacher was William Rossall, who was born on the 29th Sept., 1868, and died on the 11th Sept., 1949. He was never lonely while he had his Bible. His son, Bramwell Rossall is carrying on in his father's footsteps. He is a local preacher in the Penwortham district.

And at present carrying the torch of Wesleyan Methodism very efficiently is John Duncan Curwen, who has been serving the cause as a local preacher since 1929.

CHAPTER 13

Eagland Hill St. Mark's Church and School

THE Rev. J. D. Banister was responsible for the erection of St. Mark's Mission Church. Speaking on the occasion of his being presented with an Illuminated Testimonial and a purse of five hundred guineas after fifty-one years service, on the 13th December, 1875, Rev. J. D. Banister said : " The first services in that neighbourhood (Eagland Hill) were commenced more than forty years ago." He was then, he said, ". in the habit of going sometimes to one farm house and sometimes to another in that wide district, holding cottage lectures."

When his son, Rev. E. D. Banister, came home he helped him to have the Mission Church erected and acted as his Curate until he took up the living of Whitechapel. His last Sunday on duty was 4th Jan., 1874, but he preached on several occasions later, the last being 25th April, 1876. The last occasion on which the Rev. J. D. Banister preached in the Mission Church was on 14th May, 1876.

The Foundation Stone of the Church was laid by James Jenkinson on the 13th August, 1869. A licence to celebrate Divine Service was granted by the Bishop of Manchester on the 9th April, 1870, and the church was opened on St. Mark's Day, 20th April, 1870. The Rev. H. Ware, M.A., Vicar of Kirkby Lonsdale (later Hon. Canon of Carlisle), preached the sermon.

Where the altar now stands the fire place of James Jenkinson's cottage stood. This cottage, built by James Jenkinson in 1814, was the first to be built on Eagland Hill.

Mark Fenton, who died in 1948, was the first to be baptised in the Church, on 1st May, 1870. There is in the Church a small stone vessel with a bowl shaped cavity used as a font. Rev. J. D. Banister said in the Parish Magazine that this was the font used in the ancient St. John The Baptist's Chapel in Newers' Wood. It may, of course, have been used for that purpose, but that is purely conjectural. The shape of the vessel and the fact that it has a portion of the stone of which it is made, carved so as to be inserted in the wall point to the fact that it is, or was, a holy water stoup. It may, indeed, be of Saxon origin.

The following is a list of items of Expenditure in building the Church :—

The First Choir at Eagland Hill.

Front Row, left to right–The Misses A. Banister, E. Gornall, M. A. Stafford, M. A. A. Fenton, H. Armstrong, – Parkinson.

Middle Row–The Misses M. A. Gornall, A. Parkinson, J. Brockbank, John Gornall.

Back Row–M. Stafford, Rev. E. Bannister, Jos. Gornall, W. Moon, T. Fenton, Rev. J. D. Bannister, Jos. Gornall.

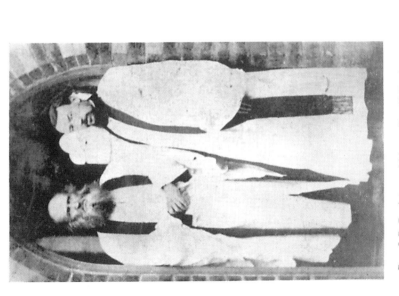

Rev. J. D. Banister and his son Rev. E. Banister.

A. Chippendale—woodwork, staining and extras ..	£74	9	4½
A. Seward—heating apparatus, iron window frames and work	71	10	9
J. Gornall, Eccleston—contract for brick work and extras	34	0	0
Sumner & Co., Fleetwood—Wood	59	5	3
A. Murgatroyd—stone and work	41	0	0
H. Moore—brick and tiles	32	12	4
Burlington—slate	23	15	2
Collinson—lead	11	12	7
H. Curwen—plasterer's work, etc.	11	3	8
J. Danson, Pilling, and North of England Iron Co. —iron	9	11	5
Boulton & Co., Staffordshire—blue bricks ..	8	6	8
London & N.W. Ry. Co.—carriage of materials ..	7	14	4
Ingleborough Works, and Ratcliffe Wharf—lime ..	4	10	8½
Cooper & Tullis—pot draining pipes	3	2	2½
Mansergh—carpet for Communion, etc.	3	0	0
Labourers work	4	17	1
R. Croft, Fleetwood—carriage of timber ..	2	8	0
Cross, Lancaster—cement	1	14	0
Foundation stones	1	13	0
Ord & Satterthwaite, Preston—hair ; Whitehead— nails	1	0	10
Lewtas, Hambleton—laths	1	8	0
Expenses at opening	5	9	0
R. Bimson—for Communion cushions and work	1	8	5
Minor bills	1	8	2
	£417	0	11½
Amount subscribed	419	10	5
Amount expended	417	0	11½
	£ 2	9	5½

The balance of £2.9.5½, together with the discount for bills and subscriptions lately received, made a sum in hand of £12.14.0, out of which had to be paid the cost of the erection of the bell and lightning conductor, and expenses incurred in lighting the room.

The value of cartage and work given was estimated at £28.5.3.

James Jenkinson, the founder of the hamlet of Eagland Hill, lived at Churchtown and walked from there when he had finished his work in the evening to Eagland Hill to build his cottage. He carried the clay in a basket from Woods Farm. He died on the 17th November, 1874, aged 88 years.

Before the present school was built there was a small school near " Tunnel Cottage." The Rev. J. D. Banister said : " It was carried on by a female, who conducted herself with great propriety. It was only a very humble school, built for the most part of clay, but it served their purpose at that time."

Afterwards it served a double purpose, for he made use of it as a lecture room, and his lectures were always well attended. Then his son " came home, broken down in health and body but in spirit as strong as ever, and he was most anxious that they should have a better school at Eagland Hill than the one they possessed." The surplus of a previous Bazaar was applied to this object and with other assistance the school was built.

The Foundation Stone was laid by the Hon. F. A. Stanley, M.P., on Whit Tuesday, 30th May, 1871. Apparently, there was a dinner to celebrate the function. Tickets could be obtained at 2/6 each.

On the first day of opening, 41 children were admitted. Of these, 28 were from the " Dame School," and some others from Pilling School. The first name to appear in the Admission Register is Joseph Jenkinson, son of William Jenkinson.

The date of erection, given by the Rev. E. D. Banister, who was the Curate and Correspondent of the school, is 4th October, 1871, although the land was not conveyed until 18th April, 1873.

The Conveyance says : " I Edmund Geoffrey Stanley Hornby . . . . do freely and voluntarily and without any valuable consideration grant and convey unto the present Minister and Church Wardens of the Township of Pilling . . . . and their Successors All that Piece or Parcel of Land situate at Eagland Hill in the said Township. (Here follows a description of the piece of land). To hold . . . . for ever. The said piece of land to be applied as a site for a Public Elementary School . . . . and for a residence of the School Master of the said School and for a Playground attached to the same School, such School to be under the management and control of the Minister for the time being of the said Township and of all Subscribers to the said School of the Annual sum of One pound or upwards."

In 1879, on the application of the Rev. J. W. Waithman, the Incorporated National Society granted £25 towards building a Teacher's house, on the condition that the School should be placed in union with the aforesaid Society and also on condition that should the said School at any time cease to be used as a school in unison with the National Society by being transferred to a School Board or otherwise alienated, this sum of £25 should be repaid to the Treasurer of the said Society.

This agreement was signed by John Wilson Waithman, Vicar, and William Shepherd and Richard Kay, Church Wardens.

In 1873 the Annual Income from School Pence amounted to £32 . 4 . 8. This was made up as under :—

Boys	Rates	6d.	4d.	2½d.	1½d.
	Number	9	4	5	3
Girls	Rates	6d.	4d.	2½d.	1½d.
	Number	7	3	4	4
Infants	Rates		4d.		1½d.
	Numbers		6		5

The different rates of payments were determined as follows :—

1st and 2nd Class.	Farmers' Children	6d.
	Labourers' ,,	2½d.
3rd and 4th Class.	Farmers' Children	4d.
	Labourers' ,,	1½d.

The salary of the Teacher was £50 per annum.

The following is a list of the Head Teachers at this school, with approximate dates only :—

Thomas Dodgson, a pupil teacher at Pilling school, was appointed master of the new school until Christmas. He commenced duties on Wednesday, the 11th October, 1871. He obtained a 1st Class Scholarship and was admitted to Battersea Training College in January 1872.

Mr. Gudhill	..	..	1872—1877
Mr. Law	..	..	1877—1884
Mr. W. Slater	..	..	1884—1896
Mr. C. Berry	..	..	1896—1904
Mr. C. Youngs	..	..	1904—1914
Mr. Robert Slater	..	..	1914—1939
Miss K. Thorpe	..	..	1939—1940
Mrs. E. A. Bargh	..	..	1940—1941
Mr. A. J. Parkinson	..	..	1941—1944
Mr. W. R. Bell	..	..	1944

James Jenkinson's Cottage.

James Jenkinson.

CHAPTER 14

The St. William's Roman Catholic Church

BEFORE the opening of this church, Roman Catholics had to attend Bonds Church at Garstang. Considerable difficulty was experienced in obtaining a site, and for twenty years efforts met with no success until Mr. Joseph Smith of Lancaster obtained the present site in 1888 and presented it to the Bishop. He also subscribed to the cost of the building. Mr. A. Dewhurst of Preston was also a generous benefactor.

The foundation was blessed by the Bishop and the stone laid on the 9th July, 1890.

The opening ceremony was performed by Bishop Bernard O'Reilly on 2nd September, 1891.

The building was constructed of Ruabon bricks, each weighing 10 lbs., and costing 1½d. each.

Several local men worked on the building, including George Cross, Peter Leach, Richard Cross, William Preston. Mr. George Cross carried twenty-four bricks (240 lbs.) in a hod to the belfry.

The construction was carried out by Messrs. J. & T. Yearsley of St. Helens.

The priests who have taken charge are as follows :—

Sept., 1891—Oct., 1900.		The Rev. E. L. Smith.
	1900—Mar., 1909.	Rev. John Smith, whose grand-parents farmed at Eagland Hill.
	1909—Nov., 1912.	Rev. Julius Maurus.
	1912—July, 1915.	Rev. Patrick O'Brien.
	1915—6th Dec., 1939.	Rev. T. Verity, loved by all, irrespective of sect.
	1939—17th April.	Rev. H. Gerrard, late Major in the Indian Army and winner of many trophies for riding.
	1947	Rev. Joseph Hardman.

The school was opened on the 5th October, 1891. The following is a list of Head Teachers :—

Miss Crudis	..	..	1891—1902
Miss Bretherton	..	..	1902—1903
Miss Beech	..	..	1903—1906
Miss Brockbank	..	..	1906—1908
Miss Helme	..	..	1908—1934
Mrs. Halpin	..	..	1934

St. William's Church.

St. William's Church, Interior.

CHAPTER 15

The Church of England School

THIS school has been known by several names—The Free Grammar School, The St. John The Baptist's School, The National, The Parochial and its present title. The story of the school commences in 1710 (1711 new style), when Robert Carter, by will, dated 31st January, 1710 (O.S.), having devised land for a school in the Township of Preesall, devised as follows : " Item. I give all that tenement in Pilling to Pilling School. Mary Mitchell shall be maintained in the tenement which I have given to Pilling School, during leases in Pilling, which I bought. I give the benefit and profit of the tenement to a teaching master at Pilling School, chosen by my executors and trustees. I give my trustees 10s. a piece out of the school benefit above mentioned, yearly, for taking care of the school." He appointed William Bell, of Pilling, trustee for Pilling tenement.

The property bequeathed by the testator was only held " for lives " and it was sold by the trustees, who afterwards purchased a freehold estate, by indenture of lease or release, dated 22nd and 24th July, 1738, in consideration of £138 . 12 . 0. The premises are thus described in the release by which they are conveyed to trustees to and for the only proper use and benefit for a teaching master at Pilling School, viz : A messuage and tenement in Pilling, by estimation, five acres, and also a field called Higginson's field, containing two acres and two falls of land, taken out of the great yard at the west end of the barn, and also a hill between the yard end of one Michael Dickinson and Henry Thompson's gate.

The original school stood, there is every reason to believe, where the Golden Ball Hotel now stands. Mrs. R. Kellet stated that her aunt, Mrs. Simpson, who died in 1898 and was then nearly ninety years of age, told her that her father (Mrs. Simpson's) said the original school stood on the spot where the Golden Ball Hotel now stands. To substantiate this, in a Lease to George Dickinson, dated 12th February, 1776, there is mention of " Part of the School field newly fenced from the sea." This could only be where The Golden Ball Hotel now stands.

Arthur Johnson was one of the first, if not the first, school master of Pilling School. A Licence was granted to Arthur Johnson, school master. He was to instruct the children at the free Grammar School at Pilling in the County of Lancaster and the Diocese of Chester, in writing and good behaviour, as well as expound to them ; ll the approved Greek and Latin authors and other texts in the vernacular tongue.

The Licence is dated 15th June, 1716. It was exhibited at the visitations of the Bishop in 1725, 1728, 1733, 1743, 1749, 1755,

The Church of England School.

[Photo by F. J. Gornall.

Broadfleet Bridge.

1760, and 1766. It was surrendered on the 17th August, 1769.

This gives us some idea of what children were supposed to know in 1716 !

The first school was a humble thatched building, with walls built of peat and stones, no doubt brought from the shore, and the floor was made of clay. In the Church Wardens' Accounts for 1803 appears the entries :—

"24 June, Thatching School 18s. 6d."

And in 1806 :

"Two load of Clay for School 2s. 6d.

Laying School floor 1s. 6d.

To wheat straw for thack 2s. 6d.

It seems, therefore, that the Church Wardens made themselves responsible for repairs and upkeep of the school fabric.

This school was burned down in 1814.

Another school was built on the site where the present school now stands in 1815. It was 30 ft. long, 21 ft. wide, and 10 ft. high.

Nothing further is known until at a meeting of the Trustees held at the Old Golden Ball Inn on 20th June, 1842, Mr. Cowan, the teaching master at that time was requested to send in an account for the last three years of the "quarterage" school fees received by him from the poor of the inhabitants of Pilling. In pursuance of which the following is a copy :—

Year	Reading	Writing	Accounts	Total
1837	£10 0 5	£4 13 0	£2 0 0	£16 13 5
1838	£14 3 8½	£5 4 0	£3 2 10	£22 10 6½
1839	£11 4 11	£7 12 2½	£3 11 5	£22 8 6½
1840	£9 13 7½	£12 14 9	£1 5 9	£23 14 1½
1841	£8 11 11	£12 19 5	£4 18 0	£26 9 4

It seems that these figures were not sufficient to satisfy the Trustees, so Mr. Cowan was requested to return a more particular account, stating the names and ages of the children.

Mr. Cowan "then stated : 24 were taught to read only at 3/- per quarter or 2½d. per week. Mr. Cowan says 3/6 when he came. That 18 were taught to read and write at 5/6 per quarter or 5d. per week. Mr. Cowan says 6/- when he came, and that 7 were taught reading, writing and arithmetic at 8/6 per quarter or 8d. per week, and no distinction between rich and poor."

The Trustees were far from satisfied. They seemed to consider the fees too high. They also seemed to realise, suddenly, "that no teaching master has been duly appointed (although Mr. Cowan had been teaching since about 1817) and that for the last sixty-two years there has been no Trustee legally authorising any appointment."*

Also, it seemed necessary to take stock of what land belonged

* A Deed of Appointment of Trustees was executed in 1841. Subsequent appointments have been made and by further deed dated 1st June, 1878, the Vicar for the time being is empowered to act in the management of the Charity.

to the Trustees. Upon enquiry, it was ascertained, " that the school estate consists of a dwelling House, Barn, Shippon and a sort of temporary stable made out of the Barn, all in tolerable repair, of about 6 acres 0 roods 24 perches of land of customary measure in the occupancy of William Calvert as tenant from year to year at the annual rent of twenty-six pounds."

At a meeting at the Ball Inn, held on the tenth day of August, 1842, it was resolved, " That the rents of the school land in future be received by Mr. Thomas Corless and by him be paid over to the Teaching Master of the school."

At a meeting held on 21st July, 1843, at the Ship Inn, the following Rules and Regulations were drawn up for the management of the Pilling *Parochial* School. (This is the first occasion on which the school is referred to by the name " Parochial.")

That in consideration of receiving the rents and profits of the school land the Master of the said school shall teach all the children of labourers and others not farming to the amount of £10 per annum, excepting persons in trade or persons having a competency for a livelihood, to read and spell correctly, and if required by the parents, thoroughly to understand the English language, and such ₁₂arents pay with each child attending the school the sum of one penny weekly. That such scholars as pay one penny per week for reading and threepence per week for reading and writing shall for the sake of distinction be called Carter's Scholars, and shall be admitted into the said school by a printed ticket from a Trustee according to the following form, viz :

PILLING PAROCHIAL SCHOOL

Admit A. B., son or daughter of C. D. of Pilling, labourer, into the Pilling Parochial School as a Carter's scholar, at one penny per week.

Signed—E. F., Trustee.

And the following Rules, to be printed on the obverse side of the ticket, shall be most implicitly observed by every scholar, viz :
1. Hands and Face to be washed clean every morning.
2. Clothes to be kept clean and dry.
3. Attendance at School and Church regular.
4. No excuse, excepting sickness, without the approbation of a Trustee.
5. Behaviour to be good both in and out of School.

N.B.—Unless the above Rules be implicitly observed, the ₁₂dmittance will be withdrawn.

And also that the following Rules be printed :—

PILLING PAROCHIAL SCHOOL
1st. This school is open to all children above six years of age.
2nd. The payment must be made in advance every Monday morning according to the following scale, viz :

Carter's Scholars or children whose parents do not farm

to the amount of £10 per annum.
Reading 1d. per week.
Reading and writing 3d. per week.
Reading, Writing and Arithmetic 6d. per week.
And for other children whose parents farm more than
£10 per annum :
Reading 3d. per week.
Reading and Writing 5d. per week.
Reading, Writing and Arithmetic 7d. per week.
N.B.—Reading includes Grammar and English History.

3rd. Books and other School requisites are found free of all charge to the Carter's Scholars.

4th. The school opens every morning at eight o'clock in Summer and at nine in Winter. In the afternoon at one o'clock, at which hours every scholar is required to be present.

5th. The religious instruction is according to the doctrines and discipline of the Church of England.

It was also agreed, " That all the Carter's Scholars do attend Sunday School."

One wonders if, for the remission of 1d. per week, it was worth while being a " Carter's Scholar ! "

But there was to be another recompense. " That the Carter's Scholars be exempt from any contribution for fire."

To these terms the Master, Mr. Cowan, agreed and continued to teach until his death early in May, 1847.

On the 15th of May, 1847, at a meeting convened in consequence of the death of Mr. John Cowan, it was resolved by the Trustees to appoint a person to superintend the children in the Parochial School until the Midsummer Holydays, 1847, so as to make enquiry for an efficient Master. At the same time, Mr. John Cottam, of Pilling Lane, was in attendance and was called into the School, and he offered to take the management of the School until the Midsummer Holydays on condition of receiving the usual quarterage from the children and such other remuneration s the Trustees had power to award to him for his services.

On the 28th June, 1847, it was resolved by the Trustees to vail themselves of Mr. John Cottam's services until Christmas, 1847, on the terms agreed on with Mr. Cottam at the meeting on the 15th of May, and Mr. Cottam agreed to teach the School on condition that the School was put in tenantable repair.

It was now felt that the school was not big enough to fulfil the educational needs of the parish, so in 1855, efforts were begun to build a new school. The Trustees—John Gardner Esq., E. G. Hornby Esq., Hy. Gardner Esq., Thos. Corless Esq., Rev. J. D. Banister, R. C. Gardner Esq., and W. Preston Esq.—promoted a subscription towards the expense of rebuilding and enlarging the school.

In memorials to the National Society and The Lords of the

Committee of Council on Education (The Ministry of Education) they state : " That this school is intended for the instruction of the children of farmers and the labouring poor.

There is an urgent need of extended education in the Township. The great number of farm labourers are not able to obtain the advantages of writing and accounts for their children at the present charges. Most of the labourers' children and also the children of the small farmers are taken from school for more than two-thirds of the year and employed in agriculture, and for the remaining portion of the year the Sunday School is their only means of education.

It is proposed to reduce the fees of the Carter's Scholars to 4d. per week for reading, writing and accounts, also 'farmers' children, to induce the parents to give the children every opportunity of improving their education. No gratuitous education exists in the Township.

There is a man, a poor cripple, who teaches a few scholars in his house, and one or two dames schools, but these charge quarter-age, in none is any particular religious instruction.

Wade (? the " poor cripple ") 30 scholars.

2 dames 15 and 10.

The present school has been conveyed by the Lords of Pilling Manor to the present Trustees, and the Lords of the Manor are willing to convey certain other adjoining wastes for a playground and a garden. The whole extent will be nearly a statute acre.

That the school is to be in connection with the National Society and is to be called The Pilling Parochial School.

Therefore, we submit the present memorial on the following grounds, viz: The want of sufficient accommodation in the present school, its present dilapidated state, also an additional school for girls and both to be used as a Sunday School as the number of scholars on the list last Summer was about 180, with 12 or 14 teachers.

The number of scholars on the list in the day school, 110 ; the attendance, 70.

The Mistress' school has only lately been established in the present Master's house, and with more convenience would no doubt have a considerable increase of scholars."

The income of the school was given as :—

					£	s.	d.
Annual Subscriptions (E. Hornby if £5, J. & H. Gardner if £5)				..	10	0	0
Collections	..	..	..		5	0	0
School Pence.	Boys	£29	12	8 .			
	Girls	£5	7	4	35	0	0
Endowment	..	..	..		20	0	0
		Total	..		£70	0	0

In a letter to the Committee of Council of Education, Rev. J. D. Banister says : " . . . . I may also state to you that the proposed school will be partly on the old site and partly on the land given for the playground and garden for instruction in husbandry to the children of all parties."

The new school was built in 1856 at a cost of £1,300. Mr. James Butler did the joinery work and went bankrupt as a result.

The Rev. J. D. Banister, speaking in 1875, said he was taken to task in the first instance for providing so large a building, but when they had secured the services of Mr. Nicholson the number of scholars gradually increased until they then had 199 in attendance.

The site on which the present school was built, including the playground, was granted " freely and voluntarily, without valuable consideration," and was conveyed by Edmund Hornby of Dalton Hall, the Rev. John Gardner of Beverly, Dr. of Civil Law and Henry Gardner of Sion Hill in the Township of Barnacre, on the 8th day of December, 1855. The Conveyance says : " . . . . grant and convey unto the Minister and Chapel Wardens . . . . that piece of ground being the site of the present school of Pilling and all that piece of ground adjoining thereto as now staked out . . . . to be used for a school for the education of Children and Adults or Children only of the labouring, manufacturing and other poorer classes in the Township of Pilling and for no other purpose . . . . and shall always be in union with and conducted according to the principles of the ends and designs of the National Society for promoting the Education of the Poor in the Principles of the Established Church throughout England."

" The control and management . . . . shall be vested in a Committee consisting of the principal Minister, his Curate, if the Minister shall appoint him, and of five other persons of whom the following shall be first appointed, Edmund George Hornby, of Castle Park, Lancaster, Henry Gardner of Sion Hill, Richard Cardwell Gardner, of Bank Cottage (later Fluke Hall), near Pilling, Thomas Corless, of Pilling, and William Preston, of Ellel Grange."

The playground went as far as Lazy Hill, and the entrance gate was there. An open dike ran through the school yard and it said the children washed their hands in the dike.

A public footpath ran past the front door of the school, but it was closed by order of the Preston Quarter Sessions dated the fourth day of April, 1855, as being of no use as the road ran close by—following a " Resolution of the Inhabitants of Pilling in vestry assembled, declaring that it to be expedient that an useless footpath in Pilling should be stopped."

In the nineteenth century it seems to have been the custom for some of the scholars to leave in Summer and return to school for the Winter months. In the Log Book, dated 7th December, 1863, is the following entry : " Readmitted the following who leave always in Summer :

James Preston	11 years.
William Jenkinson	14 years 8 mths.
Benjamin Shepherd	16 years 9 mths.
Joseph Shepherd	16 years 9 mths.
William Bradshaw	16 years 8 mths.

On the 14th December, 1863, is an interesting note : " About 30 scholars absent on the annual practice of Wheat begging, which consists in going from one farm house to another for a few handfuls of wheat and which is more profitable in the eyes of the poor parent than coming to school, it being an impossibility to make children attend school."

No doubt the poor parent would consider a little wheat very welcome when the ordinary farm worker would receive 10s. or less a week, on which to support a family.

Another custom which adversely affected attendance was that of " Egg begging " or " Peace egging." On Monday, 6th April, 1867, Mr. Nicholson wrote : " Very thin school, numbers off peace egging."

In the Parish Magazine of December, 1869, Rev. J. D. Banister writes : " We cannot close these remarks without congratulating the Parish upon the yearly decay of certain customs which yet materially interfere with the order, regularity of attendance and instruction of the children. A few years ago the school was almost emptied at ' Peace Egging ' and ' Soulmass-caking ' time. That much requires to be done yet may be seen from the following statistics :—

Soulmass Caking Time, 1868.

	Number on books		Number absent
Stds. VI and V	44	..	.. 4
Std. IV	36	..	.. 8
„ iII	52	..	.. 18
„ II	36	..	.. 10
I and under 6 yrs.	53	..	.. 25
	221		65

We shall see that about 25 per cent or one-fourth of the scholars were absent."

Here again, a few eggs would be very welcome to the working classes at a time when 1s. was paid " for ridding snow in Chapel Lane " and 6d. for " Fencing Chapel Yard," and 9d. " For carting rough cast to Chapel."

In spite of these groans, on December 7th, 1885, 227 children were present. The Staff, at that time, consisted of Mr. Nicholson (Certificated Teacher), a woman assistant to take the Infant Class and sewing, and in addition two or three " Pupil Teachers " who were not supposed to teach more than twenty-five hours a week, and, by the way, pupil teachers had to be at school at 8 a.m. to receive instruction by the Head Teacher.

Teachers' salaries were not high. To quote the figures for 1875 : Mr. Nicholson received £36 . 10 . 0 plus what other emoluments he could get ; Henry Roberts (5th year) £20 . 0 . 0 ; Thomas Winchester (3rd year) £15 . 0 . 0 ; John Winchester (1st year) £10 . 0 . 0 ; Mrs. Nicholson, 44 weeks at 3/- per week, £6 . 12 . 6.

By the Education Act of 1891 school fees were abolished. This did away with the payment of " School Pence."

At the end of the room which runs North and South was a gallery on which the children sat. It is said that, sometimes, when boys were naughty, they were shut up under the gallery, but this was not regarded as a punishment as the children sitting on the seats above pushed pencils through the cracks and the boys below got them so there must have been great competition as to who should be shut up.

This gallery was removed and a new Infant room built and opened on 27th February, 1893. The building of the Infant room was commenced in April, 1892. There was a small gallery in the Infant room. This was taken down on 29th Sept., 1906, to meet the suggestion of His Majesty's Inspector.

In the year 1904, when the new " Golden Ball " hotel was built by Major Hornby, he gave the land at the back of the school for the boys' playground, and both yards were enclosed by a wall built with stones from the old Wesleyan Chapel.

THE HEAD MASTERS OF PILLING SCHOOL.

It is very remarkable how the majority of the School Masters remained at their posts for such long periods. What was the reason ? Did they take for their maxim the old proverb, " Stick to your bush " ? Or did their roots become embedded in the soil ? Something very powerful must have held them.

The first School Master of whom there is any record was Arthur Johnson. He held his Licence from the 25th June, 1716, until 17th August, 1769. A period of fifty-three years ! He was buried in Pilling churchyard on 30th January, 1770, and his wife, Bridget, 1st June, 1775. His signature appears on many documents and Wills, so it would appear that he was " The handle of the village pump." He must have been well educated as he had to expound to the children " all the approved Greek and Latin authors."

Richard Noar, School Master, was buried here on the 28th February, 1780.

The next of whom we have any record was John Cowan. He was appointed about the year 1817. His signature, too, appears on Legal Deeds. He served until his death early in May, 1847. He is buried in the old portion of the church yard, near the South wall. He married Hannah Curwen, cousin of Henry Curwen, grandfather of Luther Curwen.

Mr. John Cottam, Pilling Lane, took charge on the 15th May, 1847. He remained until 19th June, 1852. A mere five years !

Mr. Puliston followed and remained only until January or February, 1853.

Mr. McKenzie commenced teaching on the 28th March, 1853, and remained until 2nd November, 1860. He was Head Master when the new school was opened. He and Mrs. McKenzie taught Mrs. Moss, sister of Mrs. Pearson, the late Vicar's wife. She was one of the first pupils and was very proud of the fact.

Mr. Thomas Nicholson commenced duties on the 1st January, 1861, and resigned on the 12th November, 1892. He was Choir Master and Organist for many years. On his retirement he was presented with a valuable Testimonial, executed by Shrigley and Hunt of Lancaster, and a purse of gold (£45). He was born in Lancaster and died in Cardiff on the 6th December, 1918, aged 76 years.

Mr. Thomas Richards took charge of the school on the 21st November, 1892, and ceased duties on the 31st March, 1927.

Frederick James Sobee, appointed 1st April, 1927, was educated at the Boteler Grammar School, Warrington, graduated Bachelor of Arts at the University of Manchester in 1922 and took the Teachers' Certificate in 1923, and taught in the Heathside and Parochial Schools in Warrington until appointed to Pilling.

CHAPTER 16

The Mill

THERE have been mills in Pilling—corn wind mills and water driven mills—for many centuries, very probably on or near the present site, as it is the most suitable. In the year 1242 a dispute arose between the Abbot and Convent of Leicester, which was at Cockerham, and the Abbot and Convent of Cockersand. It is stated, " The Abbot of Leicester has forgiven to the Abbot of Cockersand the demolition of two houses, the remeasurement of the pasture land between Wrampool and Pilling." On the part of the Abbot of Cockersand it was set forth, " That the Abbot and Convent of Leicester had erected a water corn mill and mill pool to the injury of their common of Garstang."

From this it would appear, since Pilling Water is the only stream, the damming of which would cause injury to the common of Garstang, that the mill was on or near the present site, that is in the year 1242. Damside, of course, owes its name to the dam. In the Registers we find the entry : " Wm., son of Richard Johnes of Damside, 22nd September, 1652."

In an Indenture between Roger Hesketh and Thomas Bell, dated 26th August, 1710, Thomas Bell agrees to bring or cause to be brought, all his corn and malt to be ground at the water mill situate in Pilling.

Next in a Deed of Division between Richard Tomlinson of Pilling and Robert Whiteside, dated 13th February, 1764, it says : " They the said Richard Tomlinson and Robert Whiteside, their heirs and assigns, always keeping twenty roods at least from the out or sea fence and also one full third part in three equal parts to be divided of all that one water corn mill and likewise all that windy corn mill situate standing and being at Pilling."

So there were then two corn mills. This is borne out by Yates' map of 1786, which shows both a wind and a water mill. The water mill is shown on the South side of the road and the wind mill on the North, near Pilling Bridge.

More than five hundred years after the Abbot of Cockersand had complained that the erection of a water corn mill had caused injury to their common of Garstang, the same complaint arose.

The most noble Archibald, Duke of Hamilton, John Trafford of Trafford House and Peter Patten of Bank and several other persons, owners of land in Pilling and the adjoining Townships of Winmarleigh and Nateby, made a complaint to the owners of the mill, viz. the Rev. Geoffrey Hornby of Winwick, Richard Tomlinson and Robert Whiteside, Gentlemen, both of Pilling, on 28th September, 1817, that their lands were being damaged by the overflow of the water of Pilling Water occasioned by a wear across the same for the purpose of conveying water to a certain water corn mill called Pilling Mill. They offered to pay a sum of £1,060 if the owners would take down the wear and would not obstruct the running water. This was done.

The cutting which conveyed the water ran from the Elletson Arms wood due North through Mr. Butler's fields and can still be seen. It must have been of long standing.

The present mill was built, in 1808, by Ralph Slater, who built several other mills in the Fylde. It is said he built the mill in twenty-one days. It is sixty-three feet high but with the revolving dome was originally seventy-three feet high. It is six storeys high and there was a platform encircling the second storey. The drying room of the present mill is said to be the same as used by the former water mill.

There were different kinds of mill stones used for grinding different materials. They were so beautifully balanced that a shaving could be taken off a sixpence.

The sails were fitted with " governors " to regulate the speed and prevent the bearings running too hot. This was a necessary precaution as mills were sometimes set on fire through the bearings becoming red hot in a storm. Cockerham mill was burned down in this way. The wind vanes were made to open and shut. When open they would offer less resistance to the wind.

In 1886 the mill was converted to steam and the sails taken down. It is sometimes said they were blown down by a storm, but that is not so. There was definitely a terrific storm, but it was the dome which was blown off, not the sails.

Describing the storm, Mrs. R. J. Palmer (formerly Miss Hannah Rossall, daughter of Mr. Elimilech Rossall) says : " I remember it so well. One of the worst I remember. The tide came over the bridge and down the hill towards the mill. The storm came in the night and my father had ropes over our house (one of some cottages which were behind the mill and which were taken down in 1935, and my brothers and sisters and I had to hang on to the ropes to keep the roof on."

Mr. R. Mather Cookson, who was born at the Mill, and whose father and grandfather lived there before him, says : " The sails were not blown off. They were removed some years prior to the storm, when the engine was installed. They were shortened first but later taken down and laid in the Mill yard. Three were taken to Birks Farm, Eagland Hill, to be used as gate posts and the fourth was used as beams in the Kiln and may be seen at the present day in the shippon which was once part of the kiln. Mrs. Palmer is quite right about the storm. The Mill House was rebuilt that year, partly on the old house, which had been a water mill. Whilst the house was being rebuilt, the gable end was blown in three times. The tide came up several hours before scheduled time. This was in December. The wind was so strong that people couldn't battle against it. Three vessels were blown on to Fluke Hall sands and wrecked. During the gale, the top of the mill was lifted and carried over the embankment into Jackson's field."

The mill stopped working in 1926.

The present mill is not very old, but the site is historic. It would be a tragedy if the mill were allowed to go. What stories the old mills could tell, standing as they did, keeping guard for more than seven hundred years over the bridge crossing the river ; what stories of the people who crossed ; what stories of joy and happiness ; of sorrow, storm and stress. Would that they could talk ! The Mill is a part of Pilling. Its loss would be irreparable.

Originally called the Gardeners Arms, the inn at Stake Pool assumed its present name in 1886 when John Gardner bequeathed his share of the lordship of the manor of Pilling to his nieces, Margaret Jane and Emily Elletson.

CHAPTER 17

The Garstang, Pilling and Knott End Railway

IN the minutes of the Garstang Rural District Council (or Board, as it was called then) of the 24th December, 1863, the following appears : " A circular letter of the 24th inst. from the Solicitors of the proposed Railway from Garstang to Knott End was read requesting to be informed whether they assented, dissented, or were neutral to the proposed scheme (that is the construction of a Railway from Garstang to Pilling).

The members of the Board directed the Clerk to inform the Solicitors that ' They dissent from such an undertaking in consequence of the crossing of the line over the highways being on the Level instead of by bridges, otherwise the Board is favourable to the undertaking.' "

In spite of this objection, the Railway from Garstang to Pilling was opened in 1870 at a cost of £150,000. The originators were some local farmers, John Hayhurst, Matthew Higginson, Edward Hornby, Thomas Salisbury, James Lawrenson and others.

The first engine was called the " Hebe," an engine with a long chimney, and with no protection for the driver and fireman. It was about 12 horse-power. It was bought on the hire purchase system and ran until 1872, when it was taken away as payments had stopped. The original drivers and firemen were James Stirzaker, Richard Smith, Matthew Sutton and Jack Rhodes.

During the succeeding three years horses were used to draw the coaches until on the 23rd February, 1875, the " Union " was purchased and goods trains began to run again, and on the 17th May passenger services were reinstituted.

In 1876 the " Farmers' Friend " was acquired by an association of residents known as " The Garstang Engineering Company " on a fourteen years lease. This eventually became the property of the Company. It was nick-named " The Pilling Pig "—it is said because its whistle sounded like a dying pig. It was used regularly until 1883, when it was sold.

It was replaced by " The Hope," which one of the shareholders, Walter Mayhew, obtained from Wigan. It was really the property of The Garstang Engineering Company and was leased to the Railway.

The " Jubilee Queen " followed.

Mr. Henry Gorst, who came from Preston, was the first Station Master at Pilling and he was followed by Mr. Richard Stirzaker.

Next came a demand for the Railway to be extended to Knott

The "Pilling Pig."

The Old Golden Ball.

End. In this the people of Pilling and the Parish Council were interested and favourably disposed. In the Minutes of a Parish Meeting for 14th March, 1898, appears the following : " Mr. R. Parkinson proposed and Mr. Cross seconded, ' That this meeting is strongly in favour of the proposed Knott End Railway being made, and which is now being promoted in The House of Commons '—carried unanimously."

On the 17th January, 1899, appear the following two Minutes at a meeting of the Parish Council : (1) " That the Clerk writes to Mr. Crosby, Solicitor, for the Garstang and Knott End Railway, stating that a station for passengers placed at Lamb's Lane would be a great convenience to the inhabitants of Smallwood Hey and its immediate neighbourhood and expressing a hope that the Company will take the suggestion into serious consideration." (2) " That the new Railway authorities be asked to place a foot-bridge where their line will cross the footpath leading from Fold Houses to Pilling Village, this being used daily by a large number of school children, to whom a level crossing would be a possible source of danger."

On the 21st November, 1899, appears the following Minute : " That the Knott End Rly. Co. be requested to place a turn gate at the point where this line, now in course of construction, crosses Ox Close Lane."

Much preparatory work was done to continue the line to Knott End—land was bought and fenced, culverts built, Preesall station built, etc., but the work had to be abandoned owing to the shortage of funds. Sir Matthew White Ridley, M.P. for Blackpool, had cut the first sod on the 25th January, 1899. In 1900 the " New Century " was bought.

Early in the year 1908 a new company was formed with a view to completing the line to Knott End. This was done and on the 1st July, 1908, the completed line was handed over to the new Company. It had cost £50,000.

The engine doing the work was the " New Century."

" The Knott End " and " The Blackpool," which were fairly modern engines, were the next and these were followed by a motor type, and latterly by the ordinary type of engine used by British Railways.

As the track was single, except where the line was looped at Pilling and Preesall, there was a special safety device used. The driver could not proceed until he exchanged a rod, which he carried, for another which was taken from an instrument in the office.

The best year recorded was 1920, when 112,000 passengers were carried. The record day was Bank Holiday Monday, when trains left Knott End every quarter of an hour between 11 a.m. and 6 p.m. The net revenue was about £2,000.

The last passenger train was run on 29th March, 1930. Mr. T. Langley, who was the Station Master at Knott End, was a passenger.

E

Mr. T. Langley was the Guard on the first train which entered Knott End station and Mr. T. Cooke, who was the fireman, drove the last passenger train.

Fog signals were laid on the line and the train arrived in Garstang Town Station with a salute of terrific explosions. Mr. W. Merricks uncoupled the last van on the last passenger train to run.

The passenger service was discontinued on economical grounds, largely caused by competition from the 'bus service.

The railway from Knott End now became a non-paying proposition, so that was closed. The last train (goods) ran on Saturday, 11th November, 1950. The key for the crossing gate at Lamb's Lane was collected from Mrs. S. Cross by Mr. J. H. Capstick, District Inspector from Lancaster. And so passes the railway into another memory.

Pilling Jubilee Silver Band around 1953. The history of a band in Pilling is somewhat obscure. The Jubilee Band was formed in 1935 and named in commemoration of the Silver Jubilee of King George V. There was, however, a band already in existence and for a short while Pilling had two bands. The date of formation of the 'Old' Band is evidently not recorded.

CHAPTER 18

Roads and Pilling Bridge

IT is possible the Romans used a track along the shore road from Cockerham and Lancaster, through Pilling and on to Preesall and Shard ford, which it is said they called Aldwath or Aldwith, which would be the nearest and best way to Kirkham. After their departure, no attempt was made to make roads until recent years.

There would be a few dangerous tracks across the Moss. Pilling was shut out by the Black Lake (Note—Black Lane Head) and shut in by the sea. Captain Dickinson, the builder of The Ship Inn, was the originator of the road by Smallwood Hey, Lamb's Lane and Head Dyke to Preesall, Stalmine, etc. This road was commenced in about the year 1780 and provided a much shorter and safer road than the shore, avoiding the danger and inconvenience of the tides and made communication with the rest of the Fylde much easier.

The road to Garstang was only made passable to traffic after the establishment of a Grain Market at Garstang in 1808. On Yates' map of 1786 there is shown a track from Cogie Hill to Winmarleigh, but there is a distinct break shown in the road from Cogie Hill to " The Island," Nateby—so called for obvious reasons. But there must have been some kind of a track, as in July, 1668, an order was made by the Quarter Sessions to the inhabitants of Pilling to repair the road on Pilling Moss between Garstang and Pilling as was customary for the inhabitants, or in default to pay £10. The repair of the roads was certainly the responsibility of the inhabitants.

In 1670 John Thornton, of Pilling, petitioned the Justices of Peace as follows (Q. S.P. 358/5) : " Showeth to your worship that a certain knowne us̀iall road to the Church mill and market Townes from Pilling called Broadfloud lying after and upon the sea coste hath beene usually repaired . . . . by severall Inhabitants within the Townshipp of Pilling upon and by the appointment of the Barlowmen (Bye-law men) there for the time being But soe it is that by the neglect and omission of the sd Inhabitants (though they have beene severall tymes warned according to custom before) have not repaired the said way soo that by their neglecte the way is in such decay and ruin that the passage there by the ffluds and Inundation of grate waters will bee shortly lost and that . . . . such as haveing occasion to passe that waie are necessitated to ryde and goe over your petioners grounds to his great losse and prejudice.

Your petioner humbly prayeth your worships order, whereby the said inhabitants may be compelled forthwith to make repair of the said waie."

On the 6th October, 1670, the Court of Sessions ordered the inhabitants of Pilling to repair the way in Pilling " lyeinge after and upon the Sea cost under the pains of ten pounds."

But the main roads of the country were in a terrible condition and that from Lancaster to Warrington was no exception, even a century later. Travelling was done on horseback and merchandise was conveyed by pack horses. Sometimes lumbering carts with huge wheels were used and these were drawn by three, four or five horses. On 7th May, 1722, '£1 was claimed for carrying soldiers and baggage between Wigan and Warrington "Ten horses Two men and Two carts."

In January, 1728, for a journey between Preston and Garstang 5/- was claimed for a cart " each cart having 4 horses the roads being extraordinary deep and bad."

In August, 1793, Thos. Buxton claimed 5s. 6d. for a waggon and five horses from Preston to Garstang, so evidently the main roads had not improved. In May, 1791, Richard Threlfall applied to the Quarter Sessions for an increase from £50 (according to an agreement 21 years previous) for surveying and repair of the 41 bridges in the Amounderness on account of the difference 21 years had made in the traffic—" At that period," he said, " few carts were made use of in the Bye ways in Amounderness Hundred in the Winter months."

By the beginning of the nineteenth century the repair of the roads began to be taken more seriously. The Surveyors of the Highways or Way Wardens, who were appointed annually by the Parish, had to see to it that the roads were kept in reasonable repair. Farmers had to send horses and carts—the number depended on the size of the farm—to cart sand to put on the roads, on pain of forfeiting for default therein the sum of ten shillings and Costs. The sand was taken from the dike at Lazy Hill, Pilling Bridge and Lane Ends.

If the roads were not kept in good repair, notice was sent from the General Quarter Sessions to the Constable to apprehend on sight and take into custody two inhabitants and take them before His Majesty's Justices of Peace furnished with sufficient sureties for their personal appearance at the next Quarter Sessions.

In the year 1822, William Bell Corless, John Dickinson, Robert Whiteside and John Tomlinson were ordered to appear, the two former on Surety of £50 each and the two latter on £25 each.

At a meeting of the Overseers at the Ship Inn on the 15th June, 1853, respecting the road across the sands to Cockerham, it was agreed that the copy of the Magistrates' Order respecting the repairs of this road be submitted to certain Magistrates in Lancaster to ascertain if possible whether the inhabitants of Pilling were liable to repair the said road with gravel and stone.

At a meeting held at the Golden Ball Inn on the 22nd June, 1853, it was unanimously agreed to resist the gravelling of the road across the sands to Cockerham, but at the same time it was agreed without a dissenting voice to keep the road in good repair with sand, " the material which has always hitherto been used for the purpose."

Mr. Robinson of Settle, Yorks, was requested to represent the Township of Pilling before the Magistrates at Garstang on the 4th day of August, 1853, against a charge for not keeping the road across the sands in sufficient repair. We do not know what the outcome was, but we do know the road was not stoned or gravelled.

On the 24th June, 1862, at a meeting held at The Gardners' Arms, Stakepool, it was agreed that the rate for the repairs of the Highways be eleven pence in the pound. It was also agreed that a new bridge be built at Stakepool.

At a meeting of Ratepayers held in The Ship Inn on the 1st September, 1877, Mr. Alderman Gardner proposed :

1. To lend £100 at the rate of £5 per cent per annum for the improvement of the sand road between Ladies Hill and Lune Bank, the Principal to be paid back in five years.

2. To give £30 towards the aforesaid improvement if the Ratepayers would meet it with £60.

Mr. Corless also proposed to give £10 towards the above mentioned improvement if the Ratepayers would accept Mr. Alderman Gardner's second proposition.

It was carried unanimously that Mr. Gardner's second proposition be accepted. It was also decided that after the expenditure of £100 in the Autumn, a portion of the aforesaid road be stoned annually by the Township. Evan Jones proposed and Robert Winder seconded, and it was unanimously agreed that a portion of the Carr Lane be stoned in the Autumn (1877).

The surfacing of Head Dyke was not carried out until very recently. It is said that when it became very bad it was levelled up with a plough.

So the Highway Surveyors and the Overseers carried on with their task until it was taken over by the Garstang Rural District Council and the Lancashire County Council.

BROADFLEET OR PILLING BRIDGE

There was probably a bridge over Pilling Water (Broadfleet) in quite early times. In 1262-68 Geoffrey de Hackensall granted to the monks of Cockersand that " their carts should pass by the sands below the bank and Hackensall Knot to his mill and so to the highway." They must either have crossed the Cocker and gone over the sands—this would not have been very easy with a heavy load—or more probably come by Higher Lane Ends from Pilling Grange and crossed Pilling Water by a bridge.

There certainly was a track over the Cocker, which came out near Pilling Hall. Mr. Rd. Mason, Mrs. M. E. Bradley's grandfather's brother, used to come over regularly to the smithy on the Cockerham shore road, which was later a Mission Room, but was eventually drowned when returning. The horses swam out at Fluke Hall.

The earliest mention I have been able to find of the bridge is in a petition to the Justices of the Bench dated 14th September, 1652, which reads as follows : " We whose names are hereunder subscribed have accordinge to your worships order of the 15th of July last viewed and considered of the decay of the Two Bridges called Broadfleet and Hawepoole (notice the spelling) and doe conceave haveinge advised with able workmen to that purpose that a fifteen and halfe through the Hundred of Amoundernesse will suffice to repayre the same, all which wee certify as uppon our owne observation this 14th of September, 1652.

> Wm. Fyfe
> Geo. Carter
> John Bradshaw
> John Taylor

Particulars of what timber will be necessary for the repair of the two bridges afforesaid :

Planks—80 planks over 50 yds. in length and four yard and half in breadth ; every plank to bee 3 inches thick.

Four wand trees sixteen every wand to bee four yards long and eight inches square.

Rayles—200 yards in length and 4 inches square.

Two head posts 2 yards long 2 foot broad and 12 inches deep.

Lastly, Posts, bands and 3 spurrs (?) which will amount to so much wood as will make 200 yards in length " (Q.S.P. 70/2).

The bridge seems to have been a constant source of trouble and expense, for on the 2nd January, 1681/2 we find that £100 was needed to rebuild the bridge, but in 1690 the bridge was in such a state of decay that a new way was recommended.

Apparently nothing was done, for on the 15th January, 1694/5 (Q.S.P. 756/3) a Petition, " Humbly showeth to yr worships that yr petitioner formerly obtained an order for the viewing of a certain place called Pilling water running betwixt Cockerham and Pilling what we have builded a bridge over the sd water but the same never being viewed nothing was done by reason whereof the sd water is now become very dangerous and almost impassable therefore that some order may be made . . . ."

It was repaired but disaster overcame it again, for on the 26th March, 1696 (Q.S.P. 777/11) several inhabitants of Pilling gave evidence that " beeing eye wittenesses of the overthrow of our Bridge and likewise being daly Spectaters of the said Bridge Before the falle thereof did not see nor perceive any fault or defect in the said Bridge before the fall thereof, neither do we believe that there was any fault or neglect in the workmen in the Building of the same But that it was only the weight and force of the flood of salt watter that was much higher than ordinary that did overthrow and Ruinate the same."

The Court was of the opinion that the work was well done and the workmen ought not to be sued.

In 1710, £4.5.4 was paid for work done on the bridge, but apparently it was down again for William Bell and Christopher Parkinson petitioned the Justices of Peace (Q.S.P. 1026/9) : " that they would allow reasonable satisfaction that whilst Pilling Bridge was down did suffer all persons having occasion to ride the road to travell through their land for over half a mile together and thereby their plowing land and meadowing very ill trodden and injured."

They were allowed £2.

In January, 1721, a wooden bridge was built for " present occasion (temporary) Passing and Repassing the mill and Market and Carr(y)ing a Horse and Load," the cost being £25.0.0.

Further work was then done and quite a substantial sum spent on it. Some interesting figures are available (Q.S.P. 1182/25) :—

Bought as much Wood and Timber for the Great Bridge in the Lords of Nether Wyersdale as amount to	57	00	00
Loading the said wood	15	00	00
Lime and stone	09	00	00
Carriage of the stone	09	00	00
Workmanship of Carpenter and Mason	30	00	00
For Pavement	02	00	00
Nails and Ironwork	02	00	00
For the second Bridge called Breck	26	00	00
The third Bridge	10	00	00

There must have been quite a flourishing little market near the Mill.

Sir Thomas Tyldesley writes in his diary under date 9th July, 1712 : " Gave Lawrence 2/6 att Pilling Bridge to buy ffish with " and on the 17th May, 1712, " Paid for 5 chicken at Pilling Bridge."

From 1722 to January, 1723, £58.9.7 was paid " To building Pilling Great Bridge and £34.19.0 to Pilling New Bridge.

There is no further mention of the Bridge until 1725, when Thomas Sheston claims 10/- (?) " for going to see Pilling bridge and the model thereof before the other bridge was begun about a dozen journeys in 2 years," which probably refers to the previous entry.

The stone bridge was built in two portions—the first was erected in the Spring of 1783.

There is an interesting letter to the Justices of Peace among the Quarter Sessions Petitions, dated the fifteenth day of January, 1784. " The humble petition of Joseph Otty Benjamin Otty and Henry Bleasdale undertakers of a bridge lately erected at Pilling that at the time of the said rebuilding of the above bridge we your petitioners delivered our estimate for getting and leading stones from two certain quarries called Pirch and the Abba both within the township of Cockerham about three miles and a half distant from the bridge in both which said places we got up a considerable quantity of stones which was not only taken from us but were severally served with writs and threatened with vexatious lawsuits which obliged us to give up the stones though we had the consent of the acting steward of the place where the stones laid and we applied to the Court at the General Quarter Sessions to give up the work but got no answer nor no relief Being thus disappointed of stones we were obliged to go to Forton Moor for the same above six miles distant from Pilling which put us to a further part more expense in leading them from the quarry above mentioned and and in this though we went into the quarry with the consent of the overseers of the town under agreement with them yet notwithstanding the consent after we had got up a quantity of stones we were not only absolutely served with writs to desist from getting stones there and the carters which we had hired and engaged for leading the same were served in like manner by which the work was much retarded and the foundation much exposed and damaged by the wash of the tide and a number of hands laid idle for want of materials to go on with besides being put to a great deal of expense in devising how to act herein being thus disappointed of stones at the proper time and the work far advanced and our work subject to the violence of the Spring tides our banks were washed down several times and notwithstanding every effort was made to preserve the same and a considerable part of the wing walls considerably more than the plan being thought not sufficient owing to the water washing deeper than we expected Notwithstanding all these disappointments and heavy losses we your petitioners have finished the said bridge to the satisfaction of our superintendent, Mr. Robert Threlfall, who can give information of our sad disappointments and losses in the undertaking which has much distressed and reduced our circumstances being poor men and therefore crave your Worships will in your wisdom and goodness consider our case and compassionately soften our loss as in your judgement shall think fit."

The initials " R.T." cut in the stone were those of Richard Thornton, whose daughter married Henry Curwen, and was therefore the great-great-grandfather of Mr. Allan Curwen and many others of that family.

The original course of the stream was through what is now the Vicarage garden where the original arch can still be seen—it is banked up on the seaward side.

The second portion was built in 1840 and the surface was paved. Apparently the reason for having one channel only was so that a greater volume of water would flow through and flush it better.

CHAPTER 19

The Enclosure of Pilling Marsh

Far above, the wide expanse of sky,
Below the velvet of the marsh doth lie ;
Bright pools left gleaming in the sun
Are jewels changing colour as the hours run ;
From opal in the noon they turn to red
As sunset throws its glow from overhead.
Gulls dip, wheel and call in intermittent tone,
And feel this wild wide territory their own.
These are the spaces all can share
So long as eyesight claims them, free as air.
Dawn, noon, the changing light and shade,
These, gladdening minds—no charge is made
To view what is more lovely I declare
Than many things far costlier and rare.

D. M. PHILLIPS

As mentioned in Chapter 3, waste land came to be regarded as the King's and the reigning monarch claimed the foreshore, in this case a vast expanse of green velvety marsh.

Pilling was undoubtedly part of the demesne lands of the Manor of Cockersand Abbey, i.e. land which the lord kept for his own occupation ; and the wastes and commons of the Manor which were used for certain purposes both by the lord and the tenants, etc.

Every Manor had its own customs relating to the services and payments to be made by the tenants. A tenant of one farm or holding might have the right to graze so many sheep or cattle or geese on the commons or unenclosed land of the Manor, or to cut turbary for his own use (not for sale). Certain tenants did graze their cattle and geese on the marsh and remove sand to sand their yards, but whether others had common rights, i.e. a right to take part of the produce of the land while its ownership belongs to another, is doubtful. They might possibly have claimed custom to take sand from the marsh.

It is almost certain that for hundreds of years sand was taken from the marsh to repair the roads. We know that in July, 1688, an order was made by the Quarter Sessions to the inhabitants of Pilling to repair the road on Pilling Moss between Garstang and Pilling " *as was customary* " for the inhabitants. From where would they obtain the sand if not from the marsh ? But, if, as might be argued, the sand was taken by the inhabitants as a profit

(*profit à prendre*) it could not be claimed by custom unless they could have presumed a grant from the sovereign (the Duchy of Lancaster) which is extremely unlikely.

The controversy of the enclosing of the marsh makes sorry reading, but it is the duty of the historian to record it.

There is no doubt that strangers were cutting and taking away quantities of marsh sods, and this possibly provided the spark which caused the conflagration for at a Parish Council meeting held on 19th March, 1895, the Rev. James Cardwell Gardner, who was the Chairman, stated "That one William Hall of Blackpool had cut and rolled large quantities of sods which he forbid Hall to take away under pain of prosecution on his own behalf and on behalf of the Parish Council." Yet on the 25th March, 1895, he stated that the Parish Council had nothing to do with it and it rested with the Lords of the Manor and those who had rights of pasturage.

By this time, also, the Duchy had erected a notice board on the marsh, prohibiting the removal of sand within fifty yards of the road.

The Rev. J. C. Gardner seems to have moved very quickly, for by the 19th November he had railed in the marsh—perhaps he moved too quickly—for he appears to have bought the marsh on three different occasions—March 1898, April 1899 and April 1904. In other words, he appears to have fenced in the marsh before he had bought it.

On 6th January, 1896, a very spirited Parish Meeting was held. Mr. C. McNeal complained of the great disadvantage to the public which the posts would cause. When the roadway was covered by the tide, pedestrians would not be able to reach the higher ground on the roadside. He also claimed the road had been diverted.

The Rev. J. C. Gardner replied that his action with respect to the marsh was prompted by the fact that it was being continually cut up by anyone and everyone, even on the roadside, thus endangering the highway. If the marsh were a beautiful green expanse instead of an eyesore as at present, he would be content to leave it so.

It was decided that a Resolution should be sent to (1) The Garstang Rural District Council protesting against the encroachment of the highway, and (2) The Lancashire County Council, complaining that "The marsh now being enclosed has been from time immemorial open to the public as a recreation ground and all the township has enjoyed the right of pasturage . . . ." The The reply from the Clerk of the County Council was not helpful. "I . . . . should be glad to know with what object it has been sent to me."

After the struggle had dragged on for thirteen years, the Clerk to the County Council wrote on the 7th May, 1908, "The County

Council have no legal powers to interfere with regard to encroachments on a Common, but they can compel the District Council to exercise their powers if the case is an interference with rights of way."

In the meantime, Rev. J. C. Cardwell appears to have been active for at a Parish Council held on 21st January, 1896, Mr. W. R. Curwen asked him if any summons had been taken out with respect to the carting of sand. He refused to reply.

A letter was read from the Board of Agriculture stating that " The Board have no jurisdiction to determine the question whether Pilling Marsh is or is not subject to rights of Common."

The fire seems to have died down during the next twelve months but burst forth again through the Rev. J. C. Gardner erecting notice boards on the marsh, stating that " Any person removing sand, sods or shillow from this sea frontage will be prosecuted."

The Clerk to the Parish Council wrote to the Duchy of Lancaster bringing this to the notice of the Clerk and informing him that from time immemorial the Parishioners of Pilling had without let or hinderance, enjoyed the privilege of utilising the Pilling Marsh for pasturage and for taking sods and sand and that the Rev. J. C. Gardner had caused writs to be served to a number of ratepayers for taking sand, but had afterwards withdrawn the case. He, also, asked the Duchy Authorities to advise the Parish Council what course to take to bring about a speedy settlement of the Marsh question.

The reply from the Duchy was : " I am to say that the Rev. J. C. Gardner appears to claim the soil of Pilling above ordinary High Water mark where it abuts on his own inclosed lands. The Officers of the Duchy have, as yet, had no opportunity of investigating the claim, which does not appear to affect the Foreshore, i.e. the land between ordinary high and low-water mark, which unquestionably belongs to the Duchy.

Mr. Gardner is also understood to recognise the existence of some rights of grazing and turbary over the Marsh, and with these the Duchy is not disposed to interfere, but they can scarcely be as extensive as the Pilling Parish Council allege, and must be connected with the ownership of some property in the Parish, and not exerciserable by the parishioners as such. With regard to the remainder of the Marsh, the Duchy is prepared to allow all reasonable rights of pasture and the taking of sods and sand from places where and to such extent as it will not interfere with the stability of the Marsh."

Advice was then sought of Mr. Gibson (? Lawyer), who upheld the view of the Duchy and said that the parishioners had only right on Pilling Marsh through owning or occupying land and that in the absence of any Lord of the Manor the Rev. J. C. Gardner could claim the marsh adjoining his land subject to any right enjoyed by the Township.

This did not allay the tension, in fact, matters reached a climax for at a Parish Meeting held on 27th January, 1898, Mr. James Gardner suggested that stringent methods be adopted and the posts be forthwith cut down. This was done with great gusto in the presence of a large number of ratepayers and the police. So that nobody should be the first it was agreed that all should strike after a count of three. Mr. Robert Gardner counted " One, Two, Three," and for his pains was the first to have his name taken. So, no doubt, thinking he " Might as well be killed for a sheep as a lamb," seized an axe and set about the stumps with a will.

They were re-erected and by June, 1898, the Rev. J. C. Gardner had enclosed the marsh edge along the Cockerham side from Pilling Bridge towards Hall Lane Ends.

This now brought the Garstang Rural District Council into the lists, as from time immemorial sand had been taken from a sandhole at Pilling Bridge, indeed, by the order of the Highway Surveyors. Moreover, the Rev. J. C. Gardner, going over the head of the R.D.C., had written to the Local Government Board complaining that the roads of the Township, and particularly those abutting the marsh, were in a bad condition and dangerous to traffic—this was stoutly denied.

The Rev. J. C. Gardner caused a Writ of Summons to be served on the Garstang Rural District Council for removing sand and an Interim Injunction to restrain the Council from so doing.

The counsel of the District Council sought the advice of Robert Newton of Lincoln's Inn, who advised that he saw very great difficulty in the Defendants' way and very much doubted whether they would succeed in establishing any rights either in themselves or in the inhabitants and in his opinion they would probably be defeated.

So the matter went quiet until it was reopened by Miss Marsden, Secretary of The Commons Open Spaces Preservation Society, Preston, who stated that her society would be prepared to take up the matter if they received local financial support, but no action was taken until May, 1908, when the Parish Council wrote to the County Council urging that the whole question of the enclosure of the marsh should be gone into.

The result was the County Council sent a Sub-Committee of the Parliamentary Committee to hold an Inquiry, which was held in the National School at 2.30 in the afternoon of Monday, 18th May.

The Chairman was Mr. V. R. Armitage. At the outset he stated that the intention of the Inquiry was to ascertain the extent of the grounds, if any, on which any future legal procedure could be conducted with regard to right of way. The question of the taking of sand and sods, he said was out of the scope of the Inquiry on account of the Rural District Council having submitted to an injunction obtained by the Rev. J. C. Gardner restraining them from doing so. Rights of Common too could not be discussed as the County Council had no authority to deal with them. This greatly limited the scope of the Inquiry.

Mr. J. Rossall, Chairman of the Parish Council, opened the proceedings by stating that the Parish Council had called for the Inquiry in response to the demand of the parishioners, and with Mr. Bradshaw and Mr. Corless, gave evidence as to right of way over the marsh.

Mr. John Hornby, who lived at Fluke Hall Cottages, spoke of herring and fluke fishing, and stated that in consequence of the enclosure he had had to sell his horse and cart and give up his occupation as fisherman.

Other witnesses were called and although there was an insistent demand that the Inquiry should consider Marsh rights generally, amid cries of dissatisfaction the Chairman closed the meeting.

The Sub-Committee reported as follows : " The Marsh appears to have been purchased by Mr. Gardner from the Duchy of Lancaster on three different occasions, viz. in March, 1898, April, 1899, and April, 1904, and in each conveyance to him appear, inter alia, the words ' Subject to any public or private rights ' from which it will be seen that the Conveyances were subject to any public right of way.

From the information given it would appear that the public had, for a great number of years prior to the purchase by Mr. Gardner, been accustomed to go across the Marsh to the sea to fish and gather cockles from the foreshore, and for this purpose had, when necessary, gone with horses, carts and hand-carts. Some evidence was also given that persons used to walk across the Marsh to Cockerham Sands. The principal method of fishing is by stake-nets and hand lines, the stakes being driven into the foreshore, though boats were occasionally used. In consequence of the fence erected by Mr. Gardner, the inhabitants of the village of Pilling have to go a considerable distance round in order to get on the foreshore and are practically debarred from fishing. According to the witnesses called at the Inquiry, the three roads usually used for going across the Marsh for this purpose were by Hannah's, otherwise Fanny's Bridge, Breck Bridge, Shillow's Bridge, and your Sub-Committee is of the opinion that negotiations should be entered into with Mr. Gardner with a view to his admitting the rights of public access to the Marsh at these three points and placing gates there to enable anyone wishing to go down to the foreshore to fish, gather cockles, or for any other lawful purpose to do so, and with horses and carts if required."

Rev. J. C. Gardner wrote to the County Council stating that he was prepared to demise to the Parish Council for 999 years, two ways across the Marsh to be used for the sole purposes of access to and from the foreshore for fishing and navigation at an annual rent of 1/- for each road and on the following conditions :—

1. The way commencing near Hannah's Bridge shall be for horses, carts and for passengers, and of a width of 9 feet.
2. The way commencing opposite the end of Wheel Lane shall be for foot passengers and of a width of 3 feet.
3. The Parish Council shall keep and maintain suitable gates at the points where these ways enter upon the Highway.
4. Both ways shall be suitably marked out and (if necessary) maintained by and at the expense of the Parish Council.
5. The Demise shall be drawn up by my Solicitors at the expense of the Council and shall contain a provision that I may alter the position or direction of either of the roads to any position or direction not more than 50 yards on either side of the position and direction indicated on the map.
6. Such other conditions as my Counsel advise are necessary for the protection of my rights.

The County Council recommended the Parish Council to accept the offer and so save an expensive litigation, and if the Parish Council did not accept the offer, it was resolved that the County Council would take no further action in the matter.

At a Parish Council Meeting held on 19th January, 1909, Mr. Corless submitted the following Resolution : " That this Council is unable to accept the terms as laid down by the Rev. J. C. Gardner, as they consider them of a most arbitrary and prohibitive nature and quite out of harmony with the wishes and rights of the inhabitants." This was carried unanimously, and at a Parish Council Meeting held on 18th January, the Council declined to pay for the cost of the draft agreement.

That was the swan song of the Marsh controversy.

On the death of the Rev. James Cardwell Gardner on the 26th June, 1913, the Fluke Hall Estate, including the Marsh, passed to his son, the Rev. Richard Titley Gardner, who sold it in July, 1916, for more than £18,000 and now Pilling Marsh sods are sent to all parts of Great Britain and Eire.

CHAPTER 20

The Moss

" That Wyre . . . .,
Takes Calder coming in to bear her company,
From Wolfscrag's cliffy foot, a hill to her at hand,
By that fair forest known within her verge to stand,
So Bowland from her breast sends Brock her to attend.
As she a forest is, so likewise doth she send
Her child on Wyresdales' flood, the dainty Wyre to wait,
With her assisting rills when Wyre repleat,
She in her crooked course to seaward softly slides,
Where Pillin's mighty moss and Mertons' on her sides
Their boggy breasts outlay, and Skipton down doth crawl,
To entertain this Wyre attendant (?) to her fall."
" Polyolbion " (1613) by Drayton.

With modern scientific methods it will soon be possible to date the peat fairly accurately. Until then, we must use what data we have.

If Kate's Pad is Iron Age then the origin of the peat was some considerable time prior to the Iron Age.

As the bronze axes were found near or at the bottom of the peat and the stone artifacts *under* the peat, obviously the peat first began to form at some time between the Neolithic Age and the Early or Middle Bronze Age, and from then onwards grew to form an almost impenetrable barrier, twelve to fifteen feet deep, skirting an extremely fertile plain of some three thousand acres.

The cause of the formation of the peat was undoubtedly subsidence of the land and deterioration of the climate. The theory of the blowing down of the forest by a storm thus causing the waters to be dammed up can be dismissed. Peat forms on the tops of hills, for example, on Bleasdale Fells, where there are no trees. It is simply owing to the fact that the water is held by the vegetation. Large areas of peat covered West Lancashire and Cheshire, in some places twenty feet thick.

Peat consists mainly of sphagnum, which grows out again on top of the dead plant and so keeps building up, bog moss, heather, sedges, cotton plant, rushes and aquatic plants, and the leaves and branches of trees.

At the bottom of the peat is a yellow substance known locally as " carr." It is iron hydroxide which gives it the yellow colour. The black colour of oak found in the peat is due to this metal.

Peat has a preserving action owing to it containing humic acid and so wood, bark, bones, nuts and even seeds have been preserved. It also contains some gallic acid and tannin.

In 1949, Mr. D. Walker, of the Botany School, Cambridge, carried out a pollen analysis of the peat at the site of " Kate's Pad " and supplied a very detailed report of the stratigraphy of the peat, a few details of which must be included here.

Of one boring he writes : " The basal 10 cms. of peat are composed largely of the remains of Phragmites (giant rush), but immediately above this, a band of highly humified peat, of a darker brown colour and containing wood, is interposed between the lighter phragmites peat beneath, and the yellowish, little decomposed " carr " above. This carr (the local name is used for convenience) is composed largely of birch and alder remains in a remarkable state of preservation, and extends upwards with only one break to the 78 cms. level. The break in the continuity occurs at 150 to 145 cms., which represents a band of more fibrous and humified peat. The latter contains some seeds of Menyanthus trifoliata (buck beans), but these become particularly common in the carr above. Above 38 cms. there is a marked transition to the darker more fibrous, more highly humified oligotrophic peats above. Between 78 and 70 cms. the peat is fibrous and contains fragments of Calluna (heather), the fibres possibly due to Eriophorum vaginatum (Hare's tail cotton grass) and grades off above into a darker fibrous peat containing Sphagnum leaves (Sphagnum cuspidatum) between 70 and 60 cms. Above this latter horizon there is a layer of black peat containing much wood and a good deal of Calluna, but above this again, the peat is rather lighter in colour, contains no wood, Sphagnum or Calluna in a recognisable state. At 45 cms. however, a strong band of Sphagnum-Polytrichum peat begins and continues up to 32 cms. Above this horizon, to the base of the mineral soil at 20 cms., the peat is black and presumably secondarily oxidised due to the oxygen made available by the cultivation of the surface layers."

By studying the stratigraphy of the peat it is possible to say with a fair amount of certainty, the conditions prevailing at any horizon, for example, if there is a band of, say, yellow undecomposed sphagnum, it points to the fact that conditions were so humid the sphagnum grew so fast that there was not time for it to decompose ; if, on the other hand, the peat is a very dark brown or black, it points to dry conditions, as growth of the plants was so slow that there was plenty of time for it to decompose. A more accurate method is by studying the pollen, for example, Mr. Walker says : " Between 90 and 87 cms. there is a rapid fall in the frequency of Cyperaceae (sedge) pollen, accompanied at the same level by a rise in the grass pollen curve. This suggests a dry phase in the history of the bog, as does the high Rumex frequency noted here." Thus, looking at the face of the peat at Kate's Pad as described

above, it is interpreted by Mr. Walker as follows :—

Depth	*Event*
32-78 cms.	Final oligotrophic stage—Dry phase. (Note—Kate's Pad horizon).
145 cms.	Second fen stage—" flooding " horizon.
150 cms.	First oligotrophic stage.
210 cms.	First fen stage.
220 cms.	Swamp stage.

Sometimes bogs burst and the evil-looking mass is spread over the surrounding countryside. This did actually happen to the Pilling moss in the year 1744/45.

The following is a copy of a letter from the Reverend Legh Richmond, Vicar of Garstang, to —— Leigh, Esq., of Adlington in the County of Chester. (Communicated by Edward Millward to the Philosophical Society, 28th Feb., 1744/45).

Dear Sir,

As you will probably hear that this neighbourhood is greatly alarmed with what they call a miracle, it may not be unacceptable if I give you the History of it.

On Saturday, January 28th, 1744 (45), Pilling Moss was observed to rise to a surprising height ; after a short time it sunk as much below the level, and moved slowly towards the south side ; in half an hour's time it covered twenty acres of land. The improved land adjoining that part of the moss which moves in a concave circle, containing nearly a hundred acres, is well nigh filled up with moss and water, in some parts it is thought to be five yards deep. A family is driven out of their dwelling house, which is quite surrounded and the fabric tumbling. The part of the moss, which is sunk like the bed of a river, runs north and south, is above a mile in length and nearly half-a-mile in breadth, so that it seems there is a continual current to the south. A man was going over the moss when it began to move ; as he was going eastward he perceived to his great astonishment that the ground under his feet moved southward. He turned back speedily and had the good fortune to escape being swallowed up. I have been at the moss to make observations every day this week. If anything happens worth your knowledge you may depend upon hearing from

Sir,

Your very affectionate
Humble Servant,

L. Richmond.

This burst must have occurred in the southern part of the bog. Mr. Walker says : " Considerations of the stratigraphy in the Pilling district . . . . show no evidence that such bursts have occurred here," and the author, who has examined the peat in company with Mr. Walker, is of the same opinion. As mentioned in the Report on Kate's Pad, there was quite definitely no sign of movement there, either vertically or laterally.   There is nothing peculiar or uncommon in bog bursts.   Lack of drainage is no doubt the cause of this movement of the peat.   The water accumulates underneath in such a large quantity that it causes the peat to float.

This happened to Solway Moss on the 16th December, 1772, and an inundation occurred in Sligo in January, 1831.

An ancient log hut was found in 1883 at a depth of fourteen feet in the peat in Donegal.   Chat moss burst and a stream of black ooze flowed down the Glazebrook stream to the River Mersey and so to the sea.   It is said that some even reached the Isle of Man.

Pilling Moss will never burst again.   Largely due to the efforts of Squire Thomas Robert Wilson Ffrance of Rawcliffe, the Out Rawcliffe moss was drained in the early part of the nineteenth century.   He brought Joseph Shawcross from Earlam, where he had had experience on the Chat Moss.   As a result of draining, the peat it became more consolidated.   A hundred years ago, the Rev. J. D. Banister said it was twelve feet deep.   To-day it varies from seven to four feet deep according to the contour of the under-lying clay.

There is an old saying :
                "Once a wood
                And then a sea.
                Now a moss
                And aye will be."

Owing to reclamation and the shortage of coal for fuel, huge tracts of the moss have gone and, with the exception of the outlying parts, the remainder is fast disappearing.   The botanist and lover of nature will deplore this.

One wonders what the monks of Cockersand would think if they could come back and see how their " Black Lake " had dis-appeared in the interests of progress, a black morass, which extended from Head Dike to Stalmine in the West and the River Wyre in the South, and Winmarleigh and Nateby in the East.

It has played its part in the story of Pilling.

CHAPTER 21

Some Gleanings

FLOODS

" *Fire and water are good servants but bad masters.*"

THE sea, like a restive horse, has to be kept in check. When the high tides are accompanied by a strong westerly wind there is always danger of it bursting the sea banks. The Bay acts like a funnel and millions of tons of water are piled up and periodically it bursts its bonds and causes havoc.

The sea has been a constant source of trouble since early times. As mentioned in Chapter IV, Cockersand was suffering in 1372. Its walls were being destroyed by the waves and ever since it has been playing tricks—playing is hardly the word to use as it is more like a raging giant striving to destroy and devour. One has only to see the huge, gaping gaps torn in the banks to realise this.

We know that in March, 1696, " the weight and force of the flood of salt watter that was much higher than ordinary did overthrow and Ruinate Pilling Bridge." This would be the " Red Flood," one of the highest tides of the year.

In the year 1720, a destructive flood was experienced as the following Petition will testify (Q.S.P. 1170/17) : " The humble petition of Stephen Bibby, George Bradshaw, William Sykes, Richard (Threlfall) . . . . Compsty, George Macknight, John Nore, Richard Whiteside, Edwd. Thornton, Thos. Jolly, John Mount . . . . on behalf of themselves and above one hundred and thirty other inhabitants, families . . . . suffers by a dreadful inundacion of the sea within pilling . . . .
Sheweth
    That upon Sunday and Monday the 18th and nineteenth days of December last (there arose) a dreadful tempest of wind, which falling out at the change of the moon and very (high) tides occasioned such an extraordinary flood that it broke down and washed away . . . . and sea fences and most of the enclosures scarce ever to be repaired and (carried) away great quantities of arrable land and in other places made such prodigious dam(age) . . . . (to be) . . . . repaired or made good and overflowed fifteen hundred acres of land destroying (most) of all the wheat and rye sowen thereon together with above forty dwelling houses . . . . barnes and outhouseing thereto belonging either entirely demolished or so ruinous (that) few or any of them are either left habitable or anyways useful, carrying away (most) . . . . of their corne,

hay, turfe, household goods, wearing apparell money and every
(? salt house) with great quantities of salt and numbers of catle,
sheep and that a great many . . . . escaped with their lives by
reason of the violence of the tides (? with fleeing) into the country
some preserving themselves with great difficulty by hanging by the
timbers . . . . times breast high or upwards in the water. Soe it
appeareed by the view of Mr. . . . Townsend, Richard Smith
and Richard Bisbrowne assisted with several experienced . . . .
that forty families are entirely ruined and without habitation
(? nothing to) rely on but the charity of their neighbours for lodgeing
and sustenance and . . . . dampnified as never to be retrieved
without charitable assistance and the losses . . . . thoroughly
discovered according to the best computation of the said persons
will amount . . . . As this is a case publickly knowne and such
as the memory of man cannot (prove) negligence as several mis-
fortunes may have been for which public . . . .

Yr petitioners therefore humbly pray that yr worships (will
issue) a proper certificate under yr hands and seals . . . . sad
and deplorable losses and yr petnrs. . . .

Stephen Bibby
Georgy Bradshaw
Willi Sykes
Richard Threlfell
James (Townsend)
George (Macknight)
John Nore

Normally, this should have been quite a high tide of about
29 feet but not excessively high.

William Stout, in his diary, writes : " . . . . a great wind
at the west. It was the greatest sea flood in the memory of any
man living. It was two feet higher than it was ever known. In
Lancaster it was four feet deep upon Green Area and a yard deep
in the Bridge Lane, and did damage in the town valued at £1,000.

Eight persons were drowned in Thornham Moss and remained
like a sea for four days. It beat down Cocker and Pillin Bridges
(caused) great loss in Pillin, Meols and Marton Mere and about
10 persons drowned. It is computed that the loss sustained upon
the sea coasts of this county by this flood could not be less than
£40,000, and if it had happened in the night, as it was in the two
days, many people would have been drowned in their beds. Many
poor people have lost what goods they had and (have) gone into
the inlands to beg."

In 1883 the tide overflowed the Cockerham Marsh and flooded
the cottages to a depth of 21 inches.

An extraordinary high tide and gale occurred on the night of
16th March, 1907. There is a record of this in the Minutes of the
Parish Council as follows : " On Saturday, the 16th March, a
fresh southerly wind had been blowing for some hours, developing

towards midnight into a furious gale and veering south-west to west. High tide was timed for shortly after one o'clock by which time the sea was pouring over the embankment in all directions. Daybreak revealed the disastrous effects of the gale. Enormous gaps, varying up to fifty yards in length, could be seen in the embankments and the country for miles round presented the appearance of an inland lake. So far inland as Bradshaw's crossing the flood was a depth of two feet, and but for the railway embankment, the inundation would have extended in that direction much further. Moss House and Pea Hall were completely isolated. The roads leading from the Marsh showed the effect of the rush of water in their torn surfaces and thick deposit of mud. It was some time before the waters got away, leaving, however, the pits and cattle drinking places full of sea water and rendering their use dangerous until in many instances, they had been completely emptied by pumping. The oldest inhabitant could not recall a similar storm and flood on this coast and fortunately the only loss of life was that of a few poultry and lambs."

The last occasion on which the sea broke through was during the night of Friday, the 29th October, 1927. Fortunately, the tide was not at the highest and the wind dropped before it was. As it was, a huge gap was torn in the bank at Pilling Hall. Lancaster Road and the houses were flooded and turnips and mangolds were floated off the fields and deposited further inland. Had the tide risen another six inches it would have come over Lazy Hill bridge and the whole village would have been flooded to a depth of two or three feet.

This same gale did a considerable amount of damage to Fleetwood.

The Pilling Parish Council organised a Relief Fund in the Parish and £105 . 0 . 0 was sent.

THE STONE EMBANKMENT

The Fluke Hall embankment was made in 1869 by R. C. Gardner, Esq., of Fluke Hall. Thomas Sherdley, of Sandside Farm, assisted with the whole of it. The Corless embankment was begun at Cockers' Dyke in 1875, and continued until the death of the owner, Thomas Corless, in 1888 and was later continued by his son, Thomas Corless, in 1897 and completed in 1899. It is one mile in length. Most of the stone used was brought over in flat-bottomed boats from Ulverston at suitable tides as far as possible on the shore and loaded into carts and carted off. The boats were loaded with sand for the return journey.

The workmen chiefly employed on the embankment were Thomas Ronson, who lived at Fluke Hall Cottages, and William Cross.

The present road leading to Ridge Farm was made in 1880-1881 by Thomas Corless.

SPORT

" All work and no play makes Jack a dull boy."

No doubt so thought our ancestors, for when the rare oppor-tunities for sport and entertainment arose they entered wholeheartedly into it. It is said that they even enjoyed watching bear baiting when occasionally a bear was brought to the village, but on one occasion, however, the large crowd of spectators was put to flight by the bear which, somehow had escaped, but the people returned to see the end of the fight, after the bear had been recaptured and secured.

Cockfighting has been practiced in Britain since before the Romans came, but how long in Pilling we do not know, certainly it was common in the eighteenth century. Parson Potter is known to have indulged.

Tradition says Bone Hill was notorious for cockfighting where a main took place as late as 1848. If this is so, and there is no reason to doubt it, cockfighting was carried on twenty years-three after the death of the Rev. James Potter, when the Rev. J. D. Banister was curate, which points to the fact that it was a fully recognised sport. The passing of the Prevention of Cruelty to Animals Act in 1849 put an end to public exhibitions of cock-fighting.

A less cruel form of sport came into fashion, that of horse-racing. The races were run on Old Pilling Feast Day and other occasions, and were usually run on the shore road, which was then sand, between Lazy Hill and Susketin Nook. A winning horse was named " Kettledrum." It was ridden by Richard Hornby and was bred at Bond's Farm by Mr. W. Morley.

Greyhound coursing, too, was very popular. Greyhounds belonging to the landowners were kept by the tenants until required. But " Limerick " Thornton owned the outstanding dog " Tory Boy," which was, however, bred at Stalmine Hall by John Singleton. This dog won at Altcar, and was running at its best in 1882. The coursing was held on the field behind Pea Hall and Pilling Hall. There were the Pilling Hall, Pea Hall and Moss Houses Stakes. " Cuddy " Danson was a slipper and Robert Winder, seated on a ladder, was the judge. If the dogs failed to catch the hare before they disappeared from sight the dog last seen nearest to the hare was adjudged the winner. Hundreds of people attended the meetings, but whether more enjoyment was derived from watching the dogs run or partaking of Mrs. Cookson's scouse, made with Pilling steak and sold on the field, is doubtful.

Pitch and Toss was another favourite game, played with large George III pennies. This probably explains why so many of these coins have been dug up in gardens.

But to turn to more manly sports and feats of prowess.

Bowling was very popular. The remains of one of the bowling greens can still be seen in the corner of the marsh at Lazy Hill.

Pilling has provided some of the early pioneers of cycling. The " bone shaker " type of bicycle was made at the smithy next to the Ship Inn by Joseph Danson, grandfather of Mr. Fred Danson, and Richard Gornall made the type known as " ordinary " or " penny farthing."

Races were held at the original Damside Farm, where Mr. Gornall lived. Pilling Brass Band attended and there were fireworks displays—the fireworks made by Mr. Gornall. The bicycles made a gay sight with their silver-plated spokes.

A tall man used a 56 in. diameter wheel ; a medium sized man a 54 in., and a small man a 52 in.

It is interesting to note that to-day, when one refers to the size of the gear of a cycle, that particular figure is really equivalent to the diameter of the front wheel of a " penny farthing " bicycle. For example, if a bicycle has a gear of 75 that would represent a " penny farthing " wheel of 75 in. diameter.

The star riders of the early twentieth century were Mr. F. J. Gornall, his brother Albert, and his cousin, John Bradshaw. These three youths held Amateur Athletic licences and upheld the honour of Pilling with great success on tracks in Lancashire from Wigan to Barrow.

From cycling we turn to running. No feast or gala day was complete without running events. In his day, R. O. Nicholson, son of Mr. T. Nicholson, seems to have been supreme. At the sports held on Queen Victoria's Jubilee Day, Monday, 21st June, 1887, he won the Quarter mile race, the 100 yds., the youths' 150 yds. and was second in the 220 yds. R. S. Jemson won the 220 yds. and came in second in the 440 yds.

But the next generation produced one who was probably the fastest competitive runner Pilling or even the Fylde has ever pro-duced—Levi Hall. Among his successes he won the Open 100 yds. race and the 440 yds. at Knott End and at Poulton-le-Fylde he won the 220 yds. hurdles, and at Brock came in second in the 100 yds. in a field of seventeen when " scratched " eight yards !

His cousin, John Newman Hall, was one of the fastest walkers in the Fylde. He won the mile walking race at Brock, Eccleston and Elswick, on grass, in eight and a half minutes in 1910. He could walk a mile on the road in eight minutes. When training, he walked from the village to the Manor Inn at Cockerham in fifty-five minutes, had five minutes rest and returned in the same time.

Mr. Wm. Thornton tells a good story : He and his friends went to the Knott End Sports and he entered for the hundred yards flat race. By some chance he found himself lined up for the one mile *walking* race ! However, he decided to see it through and set off with the rest. He soon took the lead and held it to win easily. His friends followed him round and regaled him with " ginger beer " and kept him fresh by squirting soda water over his head. The man who came second was very annoyed and struck William on the jaw. We are bound to relate he came in second again ! ''

Association football has been popular for generations. One of the most famous teams was that of 1906-1907, which won the Fylde Amateur Cup, the North Lancashire League (without a defeat) and the Fleetwood Medals—two cups and a set of medals in one season. The North Lancashire League included such towns as Lancaster, Morecambe, Kendal, Ingleton, etc.

Pilling has never lacked good goalkeepers. One deserving especial mention is Fairclough Hall, who in the late nineteenth century was undoubtedly one of the best goalkeepers in the Fylde. On one occasion at St. Annes, he gave a marvellous exhibition. The spectators applauded him to the skies and he was carried off shoulder high.

Space does not permit the inclusion of more of those '' Boys of The Old Brigade '' who have set so high a standard in the realm of Sport. A standard which is going to be difficult to maintain !

PILLING

The spelling of the name of our Township has varied through the ages, but the pronunciation seems to have remained substantially the same. The final '' g '' seems to have crept in about the beginning of the seventeenth century and to have become fairly well established by the beginning of the eighteenth.

The present-day spelling '' PILLING '' appears in a Quitclaim between Thomas Dalton and his brother Richard to Robert Parkinson of Faresnape in Bleasdale, dated 8th May, 1621, and thereafter settles down gradually to its present form.

Some of the forms of spelling met with are as follows :—

PYLIN	1194-1199	Theobald Walter's gift to the Canons of Cockersand.
PILINE	1273	Bounds between Rotheclyve (Rawcliffe) and PILINE.
PELYN	1292	Plea whereby the Abbot of Cockersand was summoned to answer his claim to assize of bread and ale.
PILYN	1292	Demand by King Edward of the Monks of Cockersand of their right of PILYN.
PYLYN	1364	Composition between the Abbots of Cockersand and Leicester.
PILLEN & PYLLEN	1536	Survey of the Possessions of Cockersand Abbey.
PYLLYNGE	1539	Sale of the site of Cockersand.
PILLYNG	1542	Lease to John Kitchen.
PYLLYN	1542	Same Grant to John Kitchen.
PYELYN	1542	The same.

PYLEN	1547	Indenture between William Hamelden and John Kechen.
PILLIN	1574	Grant to Edward Badley.
PILLINE	1597	Lease by John Calvert to Alles, widow of Robert Gardner of PILLINE.
PILLYN	1621	Order from King James 1st.
PILLINGE	1687	Parish Registers.
PYLING } PILING PYLIN }	1745	Dr. Pococke : " From Pyling we passed near Preesall . . . . having gone on two sides of Pylin moss or bog . . . . we saw to the West the great moss or bog of Piling."

THE FEAST

The first mention I have been able to find of the Feast is in the Church Wardens' Accounts for 1754—5/- was paid to Mr. Coulton at Pilling Feast—but there is not the slightest doubt it has been celebrated from very early times. It was probably instituted by the monks of Cockersand Abbey to mark the Festival of the Decollation of St. John The Baptist, the Patron Saint of the church on the 29th August.

Mr. Nicholson, Head Master, speaks of it as The Feast or The Annual Feast or The Annual Tea Party in connection with the Day and Sunday School. It was held in the first week of September until 1884, when it was held on the 13th August, and by 1893 it had become an established thing to hold it on August Monday, and by then was known as " The Coffee Feast," owing to the fact that the beverage provided was coffee.

Writing in the Parish Magazine of October, 1872, the Rev. J. D. Banister says : " This year a good deal of attention was paid to the decoration of both the school rooms and the whole school presented a gay appearance. Festoons of different kinds of leaves, a profusion of flowers, and a neat arrangement of various designs on the walls, helped to give a cheerful look to the interior on the Festival Day. The children assembled in considerable numbers. After enjoying their usual repast of coffee and currant cake, they devoted themselves to various kinds of amusements, and afforded as much pleasure to the spectators as they gave to each other."

Thanks to friends of the church and children, the " Feast " still goes on as popular as ever. " Pillingers,", young and old, gather from far and near to meet old friends and talk over the old times. What a happy day !

CHAPTER 22

Conclusion

THIS brings me to the end of my story. I do not claim it to be the complete story—far from it. Perhaps some future historian may continue where I have left off. Owing to lack of space, I have not been able to include many features of old Pilling, such as the Clubs—the " Oddfellows," " Buffaloes," the " Pool of Bethesda," which came into existence on the 1st July, 1786, or the Brass Band, which was first a Fife and Drum Band, formed in the year 1875, etc.

A volume could be written on notable Pilling personalities.

Pilling should be proud of the fact that it has produced two Mayors of the City of Liverpool, both of whom were natives of Pilling, viz. Alderman W. Preston, of Ellel Grange, Mayor in 1862, and Alderman Richard Cardwell Gardner, of Pilling Hall and later of Fluke Hall, Mayor in 1863. Alderman Preston was also High Sheriff of Lancaster.

Dr. James Gardner, grandson of Alderman R. C. Gardner, and brother of Rev. R. T. Gardner, was a world-famous oarsman, and won the " Diamond Sculls " in 1887, and was English Amateur Champion in 1890.

Not less famous is James Ronson, who with his wife Jennette, sailed to Canada in 1817 and established himself and his family at Ronson's Corner at Middleton. They were joined in 1841 by his sister Betty and her husband Thomas Sandham. From these great pioneers has sprung a large family of Ronsons, who are intensely proud of their Pilling connections. One of them, Mr. W. C. Ronson, is Master of the Mint at Ottawa. Another Ronson, who would have upheld the honour of his native village, but whose life was cut untimely short, was Harry Ronson, the son of Mr. and Mrs. Richard Ronson. After graduating at Cambridge University he became an Indian magistrate.

And so we could go on—first-class ploughmen, runners, walkers, cyclists, wrestlers, inventors, preachers—and William Thornton achieved fame, it is said, by being presented in his " Birthday suit " to King George IV as the most perfect specimen of manhood in the British Army. Cattle, horses and poultry bred by Pilling men have won premier awards at the Royal Show and The Crystal Palace.

Yes, it is verily a " Land of Goshen " in more than one sense, but its prosperity has been achieved by dint of hard work. Many of its farms have been carved out of the peat.

Gone are the days of candles, lamps and wells. Now electricity and piped water are accepted as commonplace necessities, although it was only in 1931 that piped water was brought to the village, and electricity in 1936—the Parish Council must be given credit for this.

Gone, too, are the " Boggarts," who used to prowl around— they disappeared with the coming of electric torches. But still remaining are the men and women of independent yeoman spirit, many of whom can trace their ancestry back three hundred years. To them and their children we must entrust the upholding and fostering of the fine Pilling tradition and spirit which has not failed throughout the centuries.

A group of founder members of the Pilling Historical Society conducting an excavation on Kate's Pad at Iron House Farm, Out Racliffe; back row from the left: Richard (Dick) Ronson, Matthew ('Maxie') Parkinson, John Cottam: front row Hugh Sherdley, Headlie Lawrenson. The photograph was taken c.1951 by the author using his favourite box camera which required glass plates and was mounted on a heavy tripod.

LIST OF SUBSCRIBERS

Alty, Mrs. E. and Family.
Armer, R., Springfield Cottages.
Aspinall, C., Wigan.
Atkinson. Mrs. M., Salford.
Banister, Canon M. H., Cardewlees.
Banister, Miss C. M. A.,
   Penwortham.
Barton, G., Bone Hill.
Billington, Mr. and Mrs. K.
Billington, Mr. and Mrs. W.
Blackburn, Rt. Rev. Bishop of
Bleasdale, Mr. and Mrs. J.
Bleasdale, Mrs. W.
Bradley, Robt., Windy Ridge
   Cottage.
Bradshaw, J., New Eskham.
Bradshaw, Mrs. M., New Eskham.
Bradshaw, Mr. and Mrs. R. A.
Bradshaw, Mr. and Mrs. W.,
   Christleton.
Brierley, B.
Brierley, Mrs. C.
Brindle, Miss A.
Brook, A.
Butler, Ben, Preesall.
Butler, R., and Miss M.
Butler, R., Preesall.
Butler, W. S., Preesall.
Buxton, Mr. and Mrs. S.
Cardwell, Mrs. T., Southlands.
Carroll, Mrs. K., Cambridge.
Carter, B.
Carter, Mr. and Mrs. G. A.
Carter, Jas., " Ennerdale."
Clarkson, Jas., Wheel Lane.
Clarkson, J. B.
Clarkson, W., Liverpool.
Coggin, G.
Collinson, J., Birks Farm.
Cookson, E. Cockerham.
Cookson, Rev. F. R., Barton.
Cookson, T., Tarn Farm.
Cooper, Rev. and Mrs. G. Macduff.
Cooper, Miss J. N., Penwortham.
Cooper, Miss M. C.
Corless, Mrs. A.
Corless, Miss C. E.
Corless, T. A. B.
Cross, Jn., Horwich.
Cross, W.
Crossland, Mrs. C., Bowness.
Curwen, Mr. and Mrs. J. D.
Curwen,. Mr. and Mrs. T.,
   " Cashel House."
Curson, Mrs. L., Knott End-on-Sea.
Danson, J. (Jun.), Momans Farm.

Danson, Miss M.
Danson, W., Middle Birks.
Dickinson, Mrs. J., Holly Bank.
Dickinson, J. I.
Duckworth, J.
Dugdale, Mrs. T., Gressingham.
Elletson, D. H., Esq.. Parrox Hall.
Elletson, Mrs. H., Parrox Hall.
Ellwood D., (Jun.), Hessle.
Ellwood, D., Fleetwood.
Ellwood, The Misses.
Evans, Rev. I. O.
Fishwick, Mrs. J., Townson House.
Fitz-Herbert Brockholes, Major
   J. W., C.B.E., J.P., Claughton.
Frith, Mrs. R. E., Fleetwood.
Gardner, J. D.
Gardner, Mr. and Mrs. S. D.
Gardner, W. C.
Gent, C., Manchester.
Gornall, F. J., (Sen.) Mapledene.
Gornall, J., Upper Birks.
Gornall, Mrs. Jas., Garstang.
Gornall, Mrs. Jane.
Gornall, J. R., Eagland Hill.
Gornall, Rd., Eagland Hill.
Gornall, Messrs., Myerscough.
Gough, H., Knott End.
Hall, J. L.
Hardman, Rev. Fr. J.
Haworth, Mrs. M., Parkers Close.
Higginson, A. T., Union Lane.
Higginson, Rev. B., Cockerham.
Higginson, Mr. and Mrs. M., Bond's
   Farm.
Hodgkinson, Jas., Moss House.
Hodgson, Mr. and Mrs. E.
Hodgson, T., Bay Horse.
Holden, Mrs. W., Ship Inn.
Holmes, W.
Hornby, T., Broughton.
Houghton, F. W.
Howson, Dr. W. G., Lancaster.
Hughes, Mrs. E., Churchtown.
Ingham, H., Houghton.
Ingham, J., Houghton.
Isles, Mr. and Mrs. J., Pea Hall.
Isles, W. D., Penwortham.
Jenkinson, Mr. and Mrs. A.,
   " Aberglaslyn."
Jenkinson, Mr. and Mrs. B.,
   Head Dyke House.
Jenkinson, J. H., Fold House.
Jenkinson, Jos., Masonlands.
Jenkinson, Jos., Moss Side Farm.
Jenkinson, Miss M., Holm Crest.

Jenkinson, T., Ribby Bank.
Jenkinson, W., Birks Farm.
Jenkinson, Mr. and Mrs. W.,
Jarvis Carr Farm.
Jenkinson, W., Union Lane.
Kay, The Misses, Throstles Nest.
Farm.
Kellet, Ed.
Kellet, Mrs. H., Thurnham.
Kellet, Mrs. M. A., Sandfield.
Kellet, Rd., St. Michael's on Wyre.
Kellet, Miss S.
Kellet, Mrs. S.
Kirtland, J., Sidcup.
Lawrenson, Mrs. A. E.
Lawrenson, Mrs. H., Bilsborrow.
Lawrenson, W., Damside Farm.
Mills, Mrs. G. A., Conn., U.S.A.
Moon, A. H.
Morley, C.
Morley, H.
Morley, T.
Morley, Mr. and Mrs. W.
Moss, Rev. J., Bilsborrow.
Myerscough, E.
Nicholson, The Misses, Cardiff.
Nield-Faulkner, Dr. S. A.
Nield-Faulkner, Mrs.
Palmer, Mrs. R. J., Conn., U.S.A.
Parkinson, W., Hambleton.
Pearson, P. S., Ridgypool.
Penrhyn-Hornby, C. W. L., Esq.,
J.P., Lymm.
Perrow, J. H.
Phethean, J., Reading.
Phillips, Miss D. M., Parrox Hall.
Platt, Mr. and Mrs. B., Layton.
Poole, Mrs. H., Out Rawcliffe.
Richardson, Mrs. P., Hambleton.
Ritson, E. M., " Ervadale."
Robinson, Mrs. E., Garstang.
Ronson, G. A., Parkhill, Ontario.
Ronson, R., Gable Cottage.

Ronson, W. C., Royal Canadian
Mint.
Ronson, J. S., Tilsonbury, Ontario.
Ronson, O. L., Tilsonbury, Ontario.
Ronson, Mr. and Mrs. J. B.
Ronson, Mr. and Mrs. T.
Rossall, A., Stalmine.
Rossall, R., Stalmine.
Rossall, R., J. P.
Rossall, Mrs. R.
Rossall, T., Cogie Hill.
Rowe, T.
Savidge, S. C., Woodborough.
Sharples, A., Walton-le-dale.
Shepherd, Mrs. E. A., " Roselyn."
Shepherd, R. G., Preesall.
Shepherd, Mr. and Mrs. B., Bell
Farm.
Sherdley, Rev. C., Bolton-le-Sands.
Sobee, Mr. and Mrs. F. A.
Sobee, J. E.
Steen, Mr. and Mrs. G. B.
Strickland, Mrs. M. E.
Sumner, R. B., Fleetwood.
Taylor, Dr. and Mrs. A. B.
Taylor, Dr. A., Stalmine.
Thompson, D.
Thornton, Mr. and Mrs. R., Nateby.
Thornton, T. E.
Thornton, S., Lancaster.
Thornton, Mr. and Mrs. W.
Vennard, H., Fluke Hall.
Wetton, Mrs. H., Whitbarrow.
Whalley, Mrs. H., Lytham.
Whiteside, H., Bluebell Farm.
Williamson, Jas., Bay Horse.
Williamson, Mr. and Mrs. C.
Wilson, Mr. and Mrs. A.
Winder, Miss K.
Winder, R.
Winstanley, J.
Youell, Mrs. E., N.S.W., Australia.

SUBSCRIBERS TO THE SECOND EDITION

Mrs. Ruth Abram - Hambleton
R. Almond - Knott End
C. M. Alston - Garstang
Miss F. Alty - School Lane
Mrs. H. Anderton - Garstang
Ian M. Archer - Thornton
Mrs. Christina Archer - Garstang Road
Brian Armer - Lancaster Road
Mr. & Mrs. David Armer - Horse Park Lane
P. J. Arrowsmith - Horse Park Lane
Dorothy Ashton, nee Jackson - Thornton

Eric Ball - Cheltenham
Alison Bamber - Leyland
R. N. Bamber - Garstang
Mrs. B. Bargh - Gt. Eccleston
Flora & Harry Barrowclough - Smallwood Hey
Eileen Bee - Lancaster Road
Mr. & Mrs. Peter Bell - Village Farm
Clare Berry - Southport
Peter Berry - Bispham
William & Edith Berry - Garstang Road
Marjory Bird - Johannesburgh
Sylvia Birtles - Much Hoole
Alan Birtwistle - St. Ives
Henry Blackburn - Out Rawcliffe
T. Blackburn - Out Rawcliffe
Penny Blair - Low Carr Nursery
R. Bonney - Gt. Harwood
Mrs. Sheila M. Boyes - Knott End
James Brannan - Thornton-Cleveleys
Stanley Brown - Lytham
Freda Brundish, nee Gornall - Hutton
Margaret & Mike Burke - Knott End
Dorothy Burrows - Wantage
Mrs. S. N. Butler - Garstang Road
Thomas Gardner Butler - Smallwood Hey Rd
Mr. & Mrs. M. Butterworth - Preesall
Mrs. E. M. Buzzard - Gt. Eccleston

Mrs. S. M. Cameron - Moss Bank
Mr. & Mrs. Richard Cardwell - Stalmine, 2 copies
Nellie Cardwell - Stalmine
T. & N. Cardwell - Stalmine
J. & B. A. Carpenter - Wheel Lane
M. Carter - West View Farm
Elliot Cartwright - Amersham
Olivia Sobee Cartwright - Amersham
Frank Catherwood - Garstang Road
Joe Cherry - Huyton

Rita Cherry - Lancaster Road
R. Cidzyn - Lancaster
John E. Clarkson - Harpenden
Margaret Clegg - Stalmine
Miss N. Clegg - Imperial College, London
R. Clegg - York University
David Coggin - Preesall
Joseph D. Coggin - Lancaster Road
Philip Coggin - Mythop
B. E. Cookson - Garstang Road
Mr. & Mrs. Cookson - Lancaster Road
Anthony Coppin - Garstang
Elizabeth A. Cornall - Garstang
Geoffrey Cornthwaite - Garstang Road, 2 copies
Michael & Evelyn Coulborn - Cleveleys
Miss Linda Couldwell - Lancaster Road
Mike Cowan - School Lane
Nicholas & Sarah Creer - Hambleton
Sheila Crighton - St. Annes
Duncan J. Crosby - Hambleton
Harry Cross - Taylor's Lane
Wendy Cross - Stakepool
Frederick D. Curwen - Smallwood Hey
Helen S. Curwen - Smallwood Hey
Mrs. Anne Curwen - Wheel Lane
Ursula J. Curwen - Burscough
Warren Curwen - Smallwood Hey
Bill Cutler - Gt. Eccleston

Robert Edward Danson - Preesall
Tony Davis - Duck Street
Alice Dennison - Garstang
Fred & Brenda Depport - Knott End
Barry Dickinson - Wisconsin
John Dickinson - Garstang Road
William J. Dickinson - Knott End
Sandra Dickinson & David Unwin - Fleetwood
Mr. & Mrs. A. I. Dobson - Smallwood Hey
Gordon Duggan - Blackpool
Theresa Dunderdale - Cleveleys

Hilda Eastwood - Poulton-le-Fylde
Valerie Eastwood-Thompson - Blackpool
Mr. & Mrs. C. & E. Entwistle - Church

Bob Fairclough - Cabus
Miss M. Fenton - Thornton
Iris Finn, nee Jackson - Bispham
Adrian Fisher - Knott End
Mr. & Mrs. J. S. Fisher - Garstang
Neil Fisher - Wheel Lane

Tony Fisher - Thixendale
Audrey Fletcher - Preesall
Michael & Jane Fletcher - School Lane
Mr. J. Fletcher - Layton

Beryl Gallacher, nee Aspden - Poulton
Mr. & Mrs. A. B. Gaskin - Garstang Road
A. S. Gaunt - School Lane
Vincent Gee - Walkden
Freda Gornall - Garstang Road
Jeremy Green - Claughton on Brock
Mrs. Dorothy Greenwood - Preesall
Brian Gresty - Forton
Mr. & Mrs. Paul Grindley - School Lane

Mr. & Mrs. W. F. M. Hahn - Hunter's Farm
Rodney & Anne Haire - Lancaster Road
Edmund Hall - Barton
I. Hall - Hambleton
John William Hall - Preesall
Howard Hammersley - Preston
Mrs. E. M. Harrison - Stalmine
Neil Harrison - Preesall
Raymond Harrison - St. John's Avenue
Robert James Harrison - Preesall
Tracey Harrison - St. John's Avenue
Ivy Hassett - Blackpool
David & Evelyn Hastings - Stakepool Dr.
Angela Haworth - Garstang Road
Chris Hepworth - Blackpool
Mr. & Mrs. P. Higginson - Out Rawcliffe
Gordon & Anne Hill - Stalmine
Alan Hirst - Fleetwood
Grace Hoole - Wheel Lane
Zilda Horn - Thornton-Cleveleys
Ted Hornby - Out Rawcliffe
A. Hudson - Kirkham
E. Hudson - Marton
Chloe Hughes - Bispham
Danielle Hughes - Lancaster Road
John & Cindy Hughes - Lancaster Road
John Paul Hughes - Lancaster Road
Kayleigh Hughes - Lancaster Road
Kelly Elaine Hughes - Lancaster Road
Sarah Jayne Hughes - Lancaster Road

James Ingham - Kirkland
Lily Ireton - Lancaster Road
J. Isles - Stalmine

Leslie Jackson - Ilfracombe
Mrs. Jackson - Pilling P.O.
Marilyn Jackson & Ian Mulroy - Preesall

A. Jenkinson - Scronkey Farm
Alan Jenkinson - St. John's Avenue
Arthur Jenkinson - Lancaster
Carol Jenkinson - Marton
Elizabeth Jenkinson - Eagland Hill
James Jenkinson - Garstang Road
M. I. Jenkinson - Smallwood Hey Road
Mr. & Mrs. Alan Jenkinson - Knott End
Mrs. M. Jenkinson - Moss Houses
Richard Jenkinson - Jarvis Carr Farm
Sarah Jenkinson - Eagland Hill
Roger Jones-Ronson - Northwich
Jim Jordan - Horse Park Lane

Patricia Keene, nee Higgins - Leyland
David R. Kellett - St. Michael's
Mr. & Mrs. Raymond Kellett - Cockerham, 2 copies
Mr. & Mrs. Richard Kellett - Cockerham, 2 copies
Peter Kevill - Smallwood Hey Road

Lancashire Libraries, 11 copies
Mrs. B. Lancaster - Smallwood Hey Road
Tom Latto - Southport
John Roy Lawrenson - Texas, USA
Stewart Lawrenson - Wray
Walter Lawrenson - Smallwood Hey Road
Eric & Monica Lee - Carlisle
Shirley Little - Fulwood
Mrs. Julie Katrina Littlewood - Preesall
Margaret Lowden - Lytham
Colin & Eileen Lynch - Little Eccleston
John Lynch - Oswaldtwistle

Alex Maitland - St. Annes on Sea
John B. Marsden - Eastbridge
Pauline Mason - Kirkham
Anne Maudsley - Gt. Mitton
Patricia McAloon - Cleveleys
Miss B. McHugh - Preesall
Graham McMurray - Hambleton
Peter & Hazel Melling - Grimsargh
Alan Miller - Hambleton
John Moore - Guildford
Alison Lesley Morgan - Eagland Hill
Sarah Elizabeth Morgan - Eagland Hill
Edward Morris - Preesall
G. W. & C. Mortimore - Bolton
Roger & Susan Moss - Duck Street
Alan Henry Mullineaux - Plumstead
Mrs. M. G. Murphy - Thornton-Cleveleys
Mrs. M. T. Murphy - Stalmine

Ian & Bernadette Parkinson - St. John's Av.
Mrs. Judith Pendlebury - Duck Street
Joseph Abraham Phillips - Garstang
David J. Pilling - Todmorden
G. L. Pilling - Huddersfield
Pilling Moss R. C. School
Alan R. Pitchers - Thornton-Cleveleys
John Porter - Stalmine
Anne Price - ex Out Racliffe
Mr. & Mrs. H. D. Pritchard - Head Dyke Lane
John Pye - Out Rawcliffe
Mrs. Marion Pye - Stalmine
Robert & Janice Pye - Stalmine

William & Jennifer Rainford - Peahall Farm
Joseph Redman - Lancaster Road
Mrs. Celia Redman - Lancaster Road
Jean Regan - Blackpool
Brian Rhodes - Longridge
Mrs. D. M. Rhodes - Gt. Harwood
Beryl C. Richardson - Bell Farm
P. & A. Richardson - Eagland Hill
T. G. & M. Richardson - School Lane
Mable Ridehough - Stakepool Drive
David & Sheila Robinson - St. Michael's
Shirley Robson - Farrington
P. W. & D. W. Roskell - Springfield Farm
M. Rossall - Poulton
Mr. & Mrs. Robert Rossall - Hambleton

John Salisbury - Nateby
Carole Sansome - Moss House Lane
John & Gillian Savage - Broadfleet Close
Sylvia Hannah Scarlett - Lytham St. Annes
Captain & Mrs. J. K. Schofield - Shawlands Farm
David Seamark - Cleveleys
Hazel Shaw - Calder Vale
John Shepherd - Smallwood Hey Road
Mr. & Mrs. J. D Shepherd - Moss House Farm
Mrs. E. Sherdley - Hassocks
J. T. & D. Singleton - Lancaster Road
S. J. Smedley - The Olde Ship
Walter A. Smethurst - Fold House Caravan Park
Karen Smith - Preesall

Mrs. Nicola Smith - Stalmine
P. A. Smith - Hambleton
Paul Sobee - Culcheth
Russell & Edna Southward - Winmarleigh
Mrs. Linda Squires - Carlisle
Mr. & Mrs. Adam H. Stafford - Bone Hill Lane
David Stribley - Cockerham
Mrs. Hilda Swinton - Staining
Heather Sykes - Lincoln

Mr. & Mrs. F. Taylor - West View
Mrs. Doreen Taylor - Longridge
Mrs. J. A. Thompson - Poulton
Grace Thornley - Roseacre
Mr. & Mrs. P. E. Tooth - Smallwood Hey
Margaret Turnbull - Knott End

Matthew Valentine - Bristol
Rob Valentine - Newark

Enid Walker - High Wycombe
Mrs. Walker - Stakepool P.O.
Tony Walsh - Thornton-Cleveleys
Chris J. Ward - Blackburn
Matthew Warhurst - St. Annes
Leonard Watkins - Blackpool
Mr. & Mrs. T. Watkinson - Garstang Road
James David Wearden - Penwortham
Mr. & Mrs. M. Wearden - Garstang Road
Pauline Wearden, nee Ireton - Penwortham
Susan Wells - Gt. Eccleston
Mrs. Jane West - Stalmine
Rev. Canon D. W. V. Weston - Carlisle
Anne Wheeldon - Staines
John Wilkins - Catterall
Eden Wilson - Broughton
James Winder - Knott End
E. Winders - Fulwood
Mrs. Anne Woodworth - Poulton
William Worthington - Penwortham
J. Wrathall - Garstang
J. J. Wrennall - Poulton
Frank Wright - Millom